LIVES OF
THE GREAT
SPIRITUAL LEADERS

Thames & Hudson

Henry Whitbread

LIVES OF
THE GREAT
SPIRITUAL LEADERS

20 Inspirational Tales

with 178 illustrations

For Edward, Thomas and Ellie

ON THE COVER
(front, left to right) Mother Teresa (photo Sherwin
Crasto/AP/Press Association Images) – see p. 82
Buddha (p. 16)
Guru Nanak (p. 58)
(back) Reading the Sikh holy book (p. 60)

Page 2: (from top, left to right) Rumi (p. 50), Gandhi (p. 74),
Mother Teresa (p. 82), Laozi (p. 12).
Page 3: Muhammad in Arabic calligraphy (p. 36),
Guru Nanak (p. 58), Jesus (p. 30), Moses (p. 8)

First published in the United Kingdom in 2011
by Thames & Hudson Ltd,
181A High Holborn, London WC1V 7QX

British Library Cataloguing-in-Publication Data
A catalogue record for this book is available
from the British Library
ISBN 978-0-500-51578-5

Printed and bound in Hong Kong

To find out about all our publications, please visit
www.thamesandhudson.com.
There you can subscribe to our e-newsletter,
browse or download our current catalogue,
and buy any titles that are in print.

Contents

BC

AD

LOOKING FOR SPIRITUAL LEADERS

'The lamps are different, but the light is the same.' Rumi, 13th-century Persian poet

You are trekking through a forest with a group of explorers. Someone shouts:

'Quick! Come and have a look at this!'

Hidden in the trees is a stone temple. You are the first to push open the door and step inside. All around you there are coloured windows, each one showing a picture of a different person. One shows a young woman dressed in armour, holding a banner. Another shows an Indian prince sitting under a tree.

'Found any treasure yet?' asks one of the explorers, pushing past.

'Looks empty to me,' replies another.

Underneath each figure is a name – Joan of Arc, Buddha, Jesus, Muhammad – and as you look at each window in turn, streams of sunlight shine through the glass, bathing you in their glow of many colours.

'Come on, let's go,' a voice calls, 'there's nothing here.' But something inside tells you there IS something here…

What does 'spiritual' mean?

This 'something inside' is your inner self (or spirit), your deepest awareness that goes beyond your normal thinking and feeling. Most of us are aware of having a conscience, a guiding instinct that tells us what is right and wrong. But it is also in our nature to have a powerful sense of wonder and a desire for meaning that connects us deep inside with the world around us. This is our spiritual side.

Throughout history different cultures have developed their own spiritual traditions (some forming religions), many of which have been inspired by the ideas and charisma of the individuals in this book. Today religious belief remains one of the most powerful motivating forces in the world, which means that these spiritual leaders continue to be among the most influential and fascinating people who have ever lived.

How does this book work?

This book looks at each of these great teachers through one particular event in their life, exploring their human feelings as well as their special spiritual insight. For example, in the first chapter we find the shepherd Moses trying to overcome his terror when he hears God speaking to him through a mysterious burning bush. A few pages on we hear the famous thinker Socrates defending himself in court against those who want him dead. Later we join the leader and teacher Gandhi as he collects dried sea salt from the beach to challenge unfair laws.

As each story unfolds we can begin to understand what it means to be spiritual. Although they come from different times and places in the world, each person seems to be pointing in the same direction. They all feel a powerful force driving them on; they all speak of the need for inner honesty in the outward practice of religion; and they all see the value of selflessness in order to open their hearts to the world around them. From ancient times to today, they all seem to be fired with the same inspiration. Yet because they often challenged the ideas of their time many of these people risked their own lives to bring us their message. Six out of the twenty were killed.

Back in the forest…

'Who's Martin Luther King?' asks one of the explorers, staring up at a brightly coloured window.

'I like this one,' says another, looking up at a kind-faced figure called St Francis surrounded by animals.

As the explorers choose their favourites and start to argue among themselves, you find yourself outside in the dazzling sunshine. The people in the windows were all very different, you realize. But there was one thing that they all seemed to share.

What was it?

MOSES

WHO WAS MOSES?

Moses lived around **1250 BC**

He was also known as **Moses the Lawgiver**, **Moshe Rabbenu** (Hebrew for 'Moses our Teacher/Rabbi'), **Musa** (his name in the Islamic tradition)

In which country? **Egypt/Israel**

Where? **Middle East**

Religious association **Judaism**

Quality **Courage**: Moses found the courage to stand up for what is right and to lead others.

Moses is shown as old and wise, with a grey beard. He is said to have lived to be 120 years old.

Moses lived about 3,300 years ago. He was the most important prophet of the Jewish people and is respected by Christians and Muslims too. Guided by God he overcame his self-doubt to lead the tribes of Israel out of slavery in Egypt and to give them God's laws, called the Ten Commandments.

The Pharaoh decreed that all Israelite baby boys should be drowned, so when Moses was born his mother hid him in a basket in the reeds by the River Nile. The baby Moses was found and adopted by the Pharaoh's daughter.

Moses was tending sheep when he heard a voice. It seemed to come from a burning thorn bush.

Moses and the Burning Bush

Moses hears God's voice in the desert, telling him to go to Egypt and lead his people to freedom. But he is an old man – how will he manage?

In a hot dry desert far beyond the great kingdom of Egypt Moses is looking for some shade. For forty years Moses has looked after sheep in this wilderness, and he has never known the sun to beat down so fiercely. He finds shade between two rocks and sits down, feeling a little dizzy. Above him the vastness of Mount Sinai rises up to the heavens.

Blinking the sweat from his eyes, Moses notices a thorn bush in front of him whose brittle branches have been turned white by the sunlight. It seems to shimmer in the heat as if it were blazing with a bright flame.

'Moses, Moses!' speaks a voice.

Startled, the old shepherd scrambles to his feet and looks wildly about him. But the voice seems to come from the burning bush.

'I am the God of your people, the people of Israel,' says the voice. Moses kneels as a sign of respect. His parents were Israelites but he was born in Egypt. Moses knows that the Israelites have been held captive there for many years, working as slaves building new pyramids. 'You must go to the Pharaoh, the ruler of Egypt,' the voice commands, 'and tell him to let my people go.'

The view today from Mount Sinai, in Egypt, looking down on the hot dusty desert.

Moses throws up his hands in despair. If he returns to Egypt he will be killed. Moses once killed an Egyptian slave-master who was beating an Israelite slave. Afterwards he was very frightened and ran for his life. Since then he has always hoped he would not be pursued and punished for it.

Shielding his eyes from the dazzling light, Moses tries to answer.

'Lord, I am just a shepherd. I can't tell the Pharaoh what to do.'

'You can do anything if I am with you,' replies the voice. 'You must tell my people that I am the God of Abraham, their ancestor.'

Moses shudders at the thought of standing up in front of so many people and speaking as a leader.

'But they won't listen to me,' he pleads, 'I'm not very good at speaking. And sometimes I – I can't get the words out.'

'Moses,' the voice says, 'I am your God. I am your inner strength. I am your guide.'

Moses sinks to his knees.

'Oh Lord, please send someone else.'

'Take up your stick,' the voice insists. 'Your brother, Aaron, will go with you. He will help you speak my words. I will send him to meet you.'

Moses collapses in the sand. His mouth is dry and he is shaking with shock. Yet he feels a strange lightness burning within him. He realizes that he is no longer afraid – he feels confident and strong. He is also aware of a shadow blocking the sunlight on his face and looks up to see his brother, Aaron, standing over him. Springing to his feet Moses hugs him tightly, with tears in his eyes.

'God has spoken to me,' he says. 'And he has sent you here. Our people need us in Egypt. We must bring them to this mountain to receive God's commandments. It is our duty, and God will be with us.'

Aaron smiles – how his brother Moses has changed! He is no longer quiet and shy, he is fired with purpose and energy.

As God's chosen prophet Moses realizes now that he can do what he has been asked, even if at first he did not know it. He is just the man to deliver God's word to the Pharaoh and to lead the people of Israel through the wilderness towards a new beginning.

The Passover

When Moses led the Israelites out of Egypt God sent an angel to 'pass over' their houses and punish the Pharoah. They baked unleavened bread (without yeast) because it was quicker. Today Jewish people remember their 'exodus' from Egypt at the Pesach (Passover) festival, by eating the same unleavened bread from a seder plate like this one.

After Moses had led the Israelites out of Egypt, God gave Moses the Ten Commandments on Mount Sinai. They were God's laws, and Moses' followers called him 'the lawgiver'.

'Do not follow the crowd in doing wrong.'
Moses

The Ten Commandments

1 Be loyal to God
2 Don't make your own gods
3 Respect God's name
4 Keep a holy day (holiday) for God
5 Respect your parents
6 Respect life (don't kill innocent people)
7 Respect marriage (be faithful)
8 Respect the property of others (don't steal)
9 Respect the truth (don't lie about others)
10 Respect differences (don't resent others for what they have)

LAOZI

WHO WAS LAOZI?

Laozi lived around **500 BC**

He was also known as **Old Master, Taishang Laojun**
  (which means 'One of the Three Pure Ones')

In which country? **China**

Where? **Asia**

Religious association **Taoism**

Quality **Gentleness**: 'be simple, be true, be selfless and
  want nothing'

• • • • •▶

Laozi with the long beard and moustache of a wise man, and his hair in
a topknot. Some legends say that when Laozi was born his hair was
already white.

12

Laozi is thought to have lived over 2,500 years ago.
He was a legendary Chinese sage, or wise man,
who taught that our lives should flow gently with
the mysterious 'Way' of the universe, called the 'Tao'
(or 'Dao').

*'The secret wisdom is this —
Gentleness overcomes hardness.'*
Laozi

◀• • • • •

Yin yang symbol. Taoists see the world as made up of a balance
of opposites – good/bad, light/dark, male/female – which they
call the yin and the yang. They try to live in a balance with these
natural opposites.

Laozi leaves the Kingdom

At the gateway to a steep mountain pass, a young man is waiting for the wisest sage in the whole of China.

Yi Xi is the keeper of the Hangu Pass, which marks the western border of the kingdom. In the distance he sees someone approaching. It is Laozi riding on a water buffalo.

Yi Xi has read about Laozi's philosophy and knows that it is valuable.

'Master,' he calls, when the famous philosopher is near, 'I beg you not to leave the kingdom –'

Laozi rides on. He has a white beard and white eyebrows and long ears.

'– for you will take away your wisdom with you,' says Yi Xi, bowing low.

The old man stops and dismounts. His silk tunic shimmers with colourful cloud-patterns.

'Master, I beg you, if you must leave us then write down what you know of the Way so that future generations may try to understand.'

'My words are easy to understand,' he says, 'yet no one seems able to understand them. This is why I am leaving. But it is difficult to speak of the Way.' He looks at the younger man. 'The Way is eternal and has no name.'

'Please, Master,' asks Yi Xi, 'will you write this?'

Laozi crossed the western mountains by water buffalo.

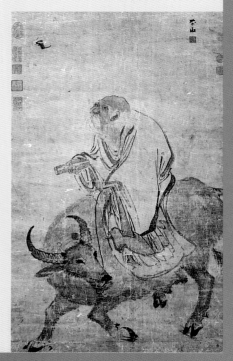

Laozi wrote two classic books called the Tao Te Ching which set out the principles of Taoism.

14

Laozi smiles at him and points to a small stream tumbling down the slope into the river below, which then winds its way down the valley.

'See how the water follows the lowest course,' he says. 'Everything follows the Way, like streams flowing in rivers into the sea. We humans follow nature, and nature follows the universe. The universe follows the Way, and the Way is the essence that determines all.' He places a wrinkled hand on the other man's shoulder. 'The Way is still, and yet it moves everything.'

Yi Xi frowns and Laozi chuckles. 'My friend, I will stay long enough to write some verses as you ask. It is good to be like water – giving and easy-going. The wise help others and reject no one. The wise are unmoved by popularity or rejection. The wise do not fret, or make a fuss, or go too far.'

The next day Laozi hands Yi Xi two sets of bamboo scrolls tied with string.

'I have written two books,' he says. 'One speaks of the Way, and the other speaks of Power.' He mounts his water buffalo. 'Remember – the Way that is spoken is not the real Way, just as any word we use is not the thing it describes.'

'Yes, Master,' says Yi Xi a little doubtfully. 'But where will you go? You have no food, no money.'

'I have three treasures,' Laozi replies, 'kindness, simplicity, and stillness. Yi Xi, just be simple, be true, be selfless and want nothing.' He begins to pick his way up the narrow path. The tall trees and the high ridges of rock hide the sun. Without turning round the old master speaks again.

'Whoever follows the natural Way leads the world –' he follows the path round a sharp bend '– carefree, calm, peaceful, at ease.' His voice trails away and he is gone.

Yi Xi is left holding the precious bamboo scrolls – the Tao Te Ching.

Laozi is never seen or heard of again.

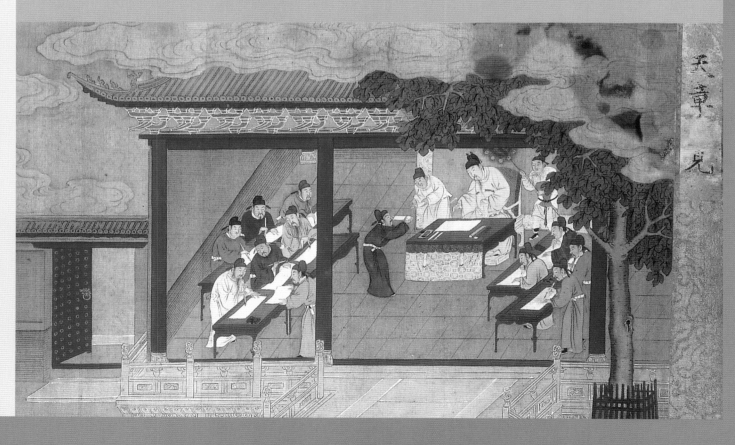

太煞隱訣

先燒香巹服礼十拜心存玄中大法師老子

河上真人尹先生回開經瘟呪曰

玄玄至道宗上德體洪元天真難遠妙近緣

泯九君宮室皆七寶窓牖目有分清淨常致

真駕景乘紫雲日月左右照外仙長年全七

祖上生天世為道德門畢叩齒卅六通咽咽

卅六過先心存左青龍右白帝前朱雀後玄

武足下八卦神龜卅六師子伏在前頭巾七

星五藏生五炁羅文覆身上三一侍經各

從千乘万騎天地各有万八千玉童玉女衛之

口設讀經五百言輙叩齒三咽液三也

道經上

道可道非常道名可名非常名无名天地始

有名萬物毋常无欲觀其妙常有欲觀所曒

此兩者同出而異名同謂之玄玄之又玄眾

妙之門

天下皆知美之為美斯惡已皆知善之為善

斯不善已有无相生難易相成長短相形高

下相傾音聲相和先後相隨是以聖人治處

无為之事行不言之教萬物作而不為始為

而不恃成功不處夫唯不處是以不去

不上賢使民不爭不貴得貨使民不盜不

見可欲使心不亂聖人治靈其心實其腹弱

其志彊其骨常使民无知无欲使知者不敢

不為則无不治

道沖而用之又不盈似萬物之宗挫其銳

解其忿和其光同其塵湛似常存吾不知誰

子象帝之先

Tao Te Ching – a Chinese book of wisdom

Laozi's bamboo scrolls contained written advice for everyday life. The title means something like 'the book of the Way and the Power'. The advice is written in a poetic style that is often like a riddle. One of his most famous lines is: 'A journey of a thousand miles begins with a single step.'

The Tao Te Ching was copied many times: this version on paper is over 1400 years old.

In the picture below, the scribes are all busy copying. The Emperor (in the yellow robe) is being presented with his own finished copy.

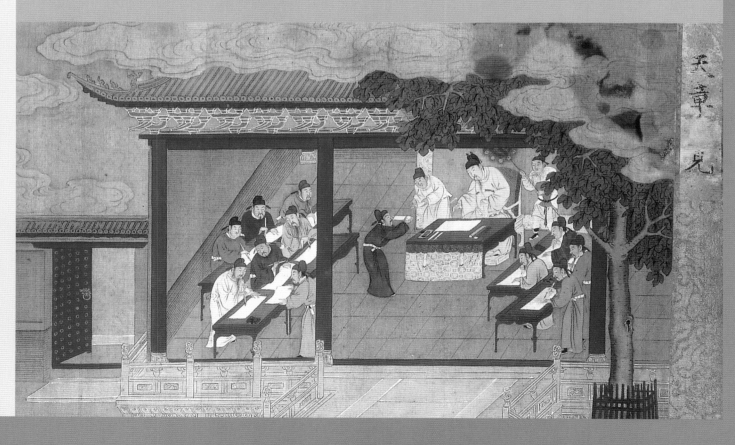

15

BUDDHA

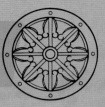

WHO WAS BUDDHA?

Buddha lived **563–483 BC**

He was also known as **Sakyamuni** (Sage of the Sakya clan), or **Prince Siddhartha Gautama**

In which country? **India**

Where? **Asia**

Religious association **Buddhism**

Quality **Selflessness**: we are not individuals, but part of a larger nature

· · · · ·▶

This golden statue of Buddha shows him meditating – thinking deeply about the meaning of life.

Buddha lived around 2,500 years ago. He was born in northern India (now Nepal), and was named Siddhartha Gautama. He gave up his life as a prince in order to find an answer to human suffering. He became the Buddha, 'the Enlightened One', and his teachings became one of the world's great religions, called Buddhism.

In a beautiful park, people gather around the Buddha to hear him talk. On the right are monks wearing yellow and orange robes who want to learn from him.

Buddha tells his friends some news in the Deer Park

Prince Siddhartha Gautama has become 'the Buddha' (which means 'the Enlightened One'). He explains to his friends what this means.

'I have something to tell you,' Buddha says to his companions. The monks are curious. They are sitting in a wooded park overlooking the river Ganges near the town of Benares in India. Deer are grazing nearby.

'I have at last found the answer,' Buddha tells them. They know him as Siddhartha Gautama, a Hindu prince who has given up his grand life in a palace in order to find a way to solve all the suffering in the world. Like them he now leads a hard life as a monk. Buddha sits cross-legged with his hands in his lap. He is strangely calm, and so the monks feel calm too.

'Two moons ago I sat beneath a Bodhi tree,' he begins, 'and I vowed not to get up until everything was clear to me. For 49 days I tried to see deeply into our human nature and suffering. Then one night by the light of the full moon I finally found enlightenment.' He looks at the others and smiles.

'My friends, you do not need to live like monks to achieve this understanding I call enlightenment. Nor should you live a life that is too soft. There is a Middle Way in all things.'

The monks look at one another and nod in understanding. Buddha continues.

'I can see now that nothing lasts forever. Everything changes or passes away, so there is no point in trying to cling on to anything. I can also see that we are all connected to each other as parts of a larger nature, which means that our actions, our "karma", have a knock-on effect on others which in turn comes back to affect us.'

'No one has to believe in gods or sacrifices. This is our dharma, our teachings. You are my first pupils, and this is the first lesson. Now let us go and teach what we know.'
Buddha

The Prince and the sick man

Prince Siddhartha Gautama leaves his palace on his horse, and for the first time in his life meets a sick man. He starts to think about suffering. He is about to leave behind his life as a prince and will soon become the Buddha.

'The way is not in the sky. The way is in the heart.'
Buddha

What is the Eightfold Path?

In the Deer Park, the Buddha explains eight rules to his friends. The Buddha draws a wheel on the ground and divides it into eight parts. 'Imagine these eight rules to follow:

1 Right understanding. Clear your mind of other beliefs and learn these things well.
2 Right intention. Give up any wrong motives and commit yourself to goodwill.
3 Right speech. Be careful to speak truthfully and not hurtfully.
4 Right action. Do not kill, steal or be indecent – be kind, honest and respectful.
5 Right work. Give up any job that is corrupt or harmful.
6 Right effort. Keep trying to improve yourself and don't give in to any weakness.
7 Right alertness. Focus clearly on your perceptions and responses.
8 Right concentration. Think deeply – detached, in harmony, serene and pure.

Learning the Eightfold Path means focusing your mind and thinking clearly.

What are the Four Noble Truths?

'I'll make it easy for you,' says Buddha. 'Let us try to understand human suffering in four simple steps – we'll call them the Four Noble Truths:

1 It is human nature to be unhappy sometimes. Happiness never lasts.
2 But our unhappiness comes from wanting things our own way. Our selfish outlook makes us unhappy.
3 We can avoid making ourselves unhappy by letting go of our selfish outlook.
4 We can let go of our selfish outlook by following the Eightfold Path.'

Buddhist monks gather together to learn the Buddha's teachings. Above their heads are prayer flags, whose colours represent different elements: blue (sky), white (air), red (fire), green (water), and yellow (earth).

Dharma (teaching): Buddha taught that we must think for ourselves.

'Do not go by what you hear,
nor by tradition,
nor by popular opinion,
nor because it is written,
nor by what seems logical,
nor by what can be deduced,
nor by appearances,
nor because it matches your views,
nor because it seems plausible,
nor out of respect for your teacher.
  But when you know in yourself that something is true, right and admirable, and leads to well-being and happiness, then live by it.'

Karma is a word that means 'actions'.

'Just as the type of seed you sow decides the fruit you will get, so good deeds will return good things, and bad deeds will return bad things. Choose your seed carefully and then taste its fruit.'

Buddha

Buddhists believe in rebirth.

After you die, you may be reborn – as a happier being (if your life was full of good actions), or as a less happy one (if your actions were less good). The final state is 'nirvana', which means 'when the flame is blown out'.

Buddha's hair is often shown tied up in a topknot, like a royal turban.

The lotus flower grows on water. For Buddhists and several other Asian religions it is a symbol of purity.

The Buddhist Code

1 Do not kill
2 Do not steal
3 Do not be indecent
4 Do not lie, or trick people
5 Do not get drunk

CONFUCIUS

WHO WAS CONFUCIUS?

Confucius lived **551–479 BC**

He was known in his lifetime as **Kong Qiu**,
  or **Kong Fuzi** (Master Kong)

In which country? **China**

Where? **Asia**

Religious association **Confucianism**

Quality **Reverence**: respect yourself,
  and others will respect you

Confucius wears traditional hat and robes, showing his
importance. He has a long beard – for the Chinese this
means he is old and wise. ······➤

Confucius was a Chinese philosopher whose wisdom
and teachings about right and wrong became famous.
He taught that good government needs people who
behave correctly, respect their elders, and treat each
other well.

Some of Confucius's lessons
were carved in writing into
seals like these ones: 'If you
know something, say so.
If you don't, admit it. That
is true knowledge.'

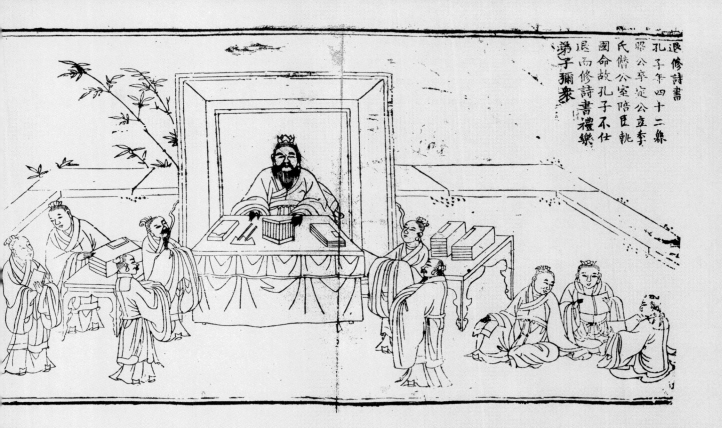

退修詩書
孔子年四十二歲
昭公章定公立季
氏僭公室陪臣靴
國命故孔子不仕
退而修詩書禮樂
弟子彌衆

Confucius talks to his pupils about right and wrong

Confucius is sitting outside his house beneath an apricot tree in the city of Qufu. He is teaching his students how to become ideal characters so that one day they may also become good government ministers.

Confucius teaches his followers outside his house. They learn that everything can be done better if one only knows the correct attitude, and can recognize the difference between right and wrong.

'The ideal person is kind because it comes naturally,' Confucius tells his students, who are gathered around in the shade of the apricot tree. 'The selfish person is kind only when it is useful.'

The 70-year-old Confucius wears his hair pinned back in a topknot beneath a traditional hat, and he has a long black beard and a long flowing robe. His students include the sons of ministers as well those from poorer families, and he accepts any gift of payment from them with a courteous bow.

Confucius has never turned away anyone who wants to study. As a boy he had to educate himself because his family were not wealthy and his father had died when he was three. He learnt all the classical poems off by heart and analysed each part of the ancient Book of Ching, so that his thirst for learning became a habit that has continued all his life.

'Even when walking in the company of two other men,' he tells them, 'I am bound to be able to learn from them. The good points of one man I copy; the bad points of the other I correct in myself.'

Although Confucius was once a junior minister he has never been given a senior position in the government and so has never had the chance to put into practice some of his reforming ideas. He even left the state of Lu for several years to see if any other states wanted his services, but few people paid attention to his advice. His students, however, are keen to learn.

'Tell us about goodwill, Master,' one of them asks.

'Love your fellow humans,' Confucius says.

'Tell us about wisdom,' another asks.

'Understand your fellow humans,' Confucius replies. The young men are silent so he continues. 'People are close to one another by nature. They only differ as a result of their traditional customs. So make this a golden rule – what you do not want done to you, do not do to others.'

Confucius likes to be correct about everything. He observes all the proper rituals and his manners are exemplary. He regularly visits the graves of his parents and teaches his disciples that showing loyalty and respect for parents is an important duty.

A messenger from the Duke of Lu has arrived and Confucius is summoned to the palace. With a solemn expression he leaves immediately, not waiting for a horse and carriage. He walks hurriedly through the streets and markets, past the bone and pottery craftsmen and the workshops smelting iron and copper until he reaches the inner city walls. On the hill stands the royal ancestral temple and the grand palace.

Confucius takes quick short steps so that in his long gown he seems to glide through the red pillars of the entrance with his hands clasped in front of him. He holds his breath as he mounts the stairs and then bows low in the presence of the Duke. A mat is brought for him to sit on but Confucius continues to stand until the servant has straightened it.

One day, he hopes, the Duke will realize the importance of orderliness and personal respect in setting the tone for good government.

How do we know what Confucius taught?

Taken from broken stone tablets that are almost 2,000 years old, these ink rubbings are made on paper to show the pattern of the writing. They are Confucius's words, written down by his pupils, telling us what he taught. They are called the Analects – 'things gathered together'.

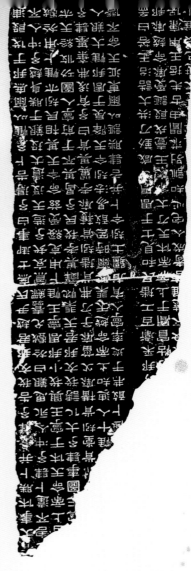

Confucius met another wise man, Laozi. Confucius told his followers, 'Birds can fly, fish can swim, animals can run, so they can all be snared or trapped. But Laozi is like a flying dragon, un-trappable.'

'What you do not want done to you, do not do to others.'
Confucius

SOCRATES

WHO WAS SOCRATES?

Socrates lived **470–399 BC**
He was also known as **The Gadfly of Athens**
In which country? **Greece**
Where? **Europe**
Religious association **Ancient Greek philosophy**
Quality **Reason:** ask questions to find out what is right
   and wrong

Socrates was famously ugly, with his snub nose, bald head and old clothes. But he was so clever that people wanted to follow him and listen to his conversations. ·······▶

Socrates was the first of the great Greek philosophers. His way of discovering what was true and good was to question what other people thought they already knew. If you ask enough difficult questions about life – What makes us happy? What makes us good? – you may get closer to the truth. But you may also find there is no easy answer. Socrates showed that sometimes it is wiser to admit that you don't know.

'The only real wisdom:
I know that I know nothing.'
Socrates

◀······
Socrates walked and talked in the agora, the meeting place in the centre of Athens. One of his followers was Plato (wearing red). Plato then taught Aristotle (next to him in blue). The three philosophers are the first great thinkers of Western civilization.

Socrates defends himself in court

There is a murmur of anticipation as Socrates stands up to speak. He is famous throughout Athens for being a clever speaker. A breeze wafts through the stone columns of the open-air Court House, carrying with it the sounds of the market outside. Spectators jostle for a better view. The water clock has been filled: now Socrates has three hours to answer the accusations against him.

Socrates addresses the five hundred jurors sitting in the Court on rows of wooden benches: 'I must confess, gentlemen,' his eyes sparkle mischievously, 'that I found myself almost agreeing with the arguments of my three accusers, they were so convincing.' He looks down from the raised stage at three men. 'But unfortunately, nothing of what they say is true.'

'Meletus here' – Socrates points to one of them – 'accuses me of inventing my own god. He also says I am a bad influence on the young people of Athens. And yet all I have ever done is to encourage people to think for themselves. When I philosophize in the agora I only question those who claim to be wise, like politicians, in order to find out the truth. I am like my mother, who was a midwife – I try to help deliver what others are thinking. If I appear wise,' he says, 'it's only because I don't claim to know what I do not know.'

Socrates was a familiar sight in the city of Athens, since he liked to talk to his followers in the open air. He loved the company of young people who were willing to think in new ways.

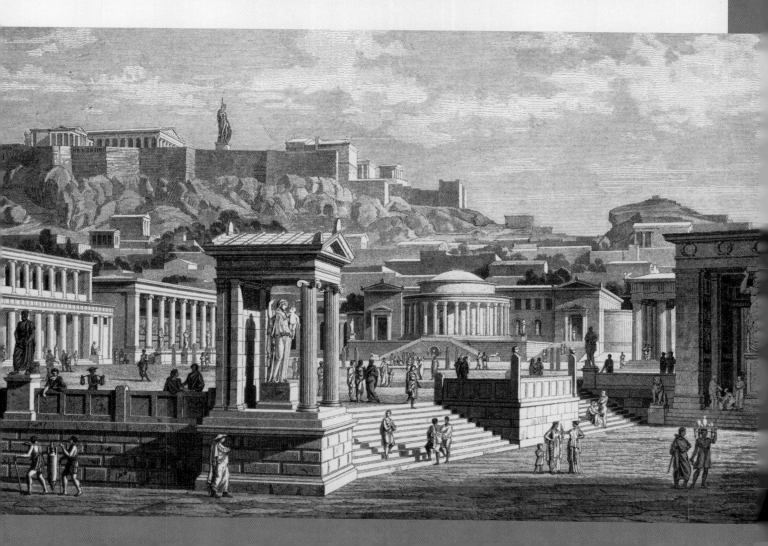

The gods of ancient Greece painted on the side of a vase that was made at the time Socrates was alive. Socrates respected the gods, but was accused of inventing gods of his own.

'To find yourself, think for yourself.'
Socrates

You can still visit the ancient *agora* in Athens where Socrates used to walk and discuss ideas with young people. His philosophy continues to be taught all over the world, almost 2,500 years after his death.

'So, Meletus, what is your argument?' says Socrates. 'Do you think I tell young people to believe in different gods, or maybe in no gods at all?'

'You believe in no gods,' a sour-faced Meletus states firmly, crossing his arms. He has long straight hair, a thin beard and a beaky nose.

'You mean to say that I might doubt the stories of Mount Olympus, home to all the gods and their little squabbles?' Socrates replies. 'I can't understand how I can be accused of believing in no gods at the same time as believing in my own. You have even signed an oath accusing me of this. Do you think I might suspect the sun and moon not to be gods but made of stone? How, Meletus, are you so much wiser at your age than I am at mine? So come along, my clever friend, what evidence do you have that I am a bad influence on people? Make him answer, gentlemen.'

Socrates smiles all around at his audience. 'Look, I can see my young friends Plato and his brother among the spectators. If they have been corrupted by me why do my accusers not call them as witnesses against me?'

Meletus is on his feet shouting objections and the spectators are jeering.

'The simple truth is this,' Socrates silences the storms of protest. 'If you let me go I will carry on discussing philosophy with my fellow Athenians, for that is my religious duty. Ever since I was a child an inner voice has told me to make the people of this great city think, like a fly stings a lazy horse.'

Socrates is about to drink deadly hemlock in his prison cell. Socrates' friends have tried to persuade him to escape but he has refused. After all, Socrates believes in reason: since he has decided to stay in the city, he has a duty to obey the city's law.

The Verdict

When Socrates sits down, each member of the jury votes. Socrates is accused of corrupting young people and showing disrespect to the city's gods. His accusers demand the death penalty, but Socrates is given the chance to choose the method of execution.

'Rather than punish me you ought to give me a reward,' Socrates replies. 'It is only by questioning what we think we know that we can clear our minds of false ideas and find out what is right. If that is my crime, I am not afraid to die for it.'

The verdict is announced: guilty.

Socrates must drink hemlock poison.

JESUS

WHO WAS JESUS?

Jesus lived **0–AD 33**

He was also known as **Messiah**
  (from Hebrew for 'the Anointed One'),
  Christ (from Greek for 'the Anointed One'),
  'Isa (the prophet in the Islamic tradition)

In which country? **Israel**

Where? **Middle East**

Religious association **Judaism/Christianity**

Quality **Goodwill**: show goodwill to all
  people, whoever they are

Jesus is often shown as a gentle and thoughtful man. ••••••➤

The lamb (shown here with a Christian banner) is a symbol of sacrifice. It is not a heroic animal either: lambs are gentle creatures that need help and support.

Jesus was born over 2,000 years ago. He was a Jewish preacher who was hailed as God's special 'messiah' or 'christ' by his followers, the Christians. He taught the importance of acting with goodwill in keeping God's laws. Instead of fighting our enemies, Jesus suggested we should treat them with love. 'If someone strikes you on the cheek,' he said, 'offer him the other cheek too.' Jesus showed that leaders do not have to be fighters to show their strength.

'Love your enemies, do good to those who hate you.'

Jesus

Faithful fishermen

The fish is a popular Christian symbol. Jesus lived by the Sea of Galilee where he met some fishermen who became his followers. He told them that instead of casting their nets for fish, they should become 'fishers of men' by calling people back to God's law.

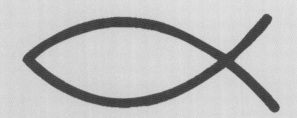

The first letter of each word in the Greek phrase for 'Jesus Christ, God's son, saviour' spells ICHTHUS, which means fish.

Jesus teaches his followers to love one another

Men, women and children hurry up the hillside from their village, eager to meet the man who people say is the long-awaited 'messiah', the saviour promised by God in the scriptures.

A young Jewish man with dark hair, a beard, and a plain linen robe is waiting for the villagers among the rocks and olive trees. His name is Jesus, and with him are his disciples (followers), simple men from near the Sea of Galilee.

'I have an important message for you,' he tells his new audience. 'God's kingdom is coming, and if you want to live forever you must return to God's Law, which is to love God and to love your neighbour.' His voice has a strange quiet power.

◄ • • • • • •
Jesus came from the town of Nazareth, on the Sea of Galilee in Judea (now in northern Israel). He used to preach and tell stories to Jews who lived here, and he grew hugely popular.

The Good Samaritan stops to help a wounded man, while behind him others hurry on their way. Samaritans were hated by the Jews, but Jesus told this story to show how people should all help each other.

Hearing Jesus speak, immediately a man in the crowd stands up. He is an expert in the scriptures (religious texts) and he wants to trick Jesus.

'I obey the laws,' he says, 'but who exactly counts as my neighbour?'

The Good Samaritan

'There was once a man,' Jesus explains, 'who was travelling on foot between Jerusalem and Jericho. On the way he was robbed and beaten by bandits and left for dead. Soon a priest came along the same way, but when he saw the wounded man, he passed by on the other side of the road.'

There is a gasp from the crowd. *A priest is a man of God – he should know better*, they mutter.

'Then a man from a good family came by,' Jesus continues. 'He was a temple assistant, and he looked at the wounded man before leaving him lying there, as the priest had done.'

The people murmur uncomfortably to each other again and Jesus waits for them to settle.

'Then who should come past next,' he says, stretching out an arm, 'but a Samaritan.' Now the villagers laugh and scoff. They despise the neighbouring people of Samaria and would not expect any of them to help a Jewish man from Jerusalem. 'And this man,' Jesus speaks above the chatter, 'felt sorry for the wounded man and dressed his wounds very carefully.'

Some of the people fall silent to listen.

'The good Samaritan lifted the wounded man onto his donkey and took him to an inn and took care of him. He then paid the innkeeper two days' wages and said, "Look after this man. If it costs more than I have given you then I will repay you when I next return here".'

Jesus turns to the man who asked the question, and says to him softly, 'So, friend, which of the three travellers do you think was the wounded man's neighbour?'

The man nods in recognition. 'The stranger who went out of his way to look after him,' he says.

Jesus smiles. Every person there hears his gentle voice:

'*Then go and do the same.*'

The Disciples

Jesus' followers are called disciples. They were his students. Jesus taught them with many parables (stories with a moral or lesson) like the one about the Good Samaritan.

Jesus showed his disciples that being gentle, humble and honest was not only the best way to live, but also the best way to be strong. He showed how powerful a quiet leader can be.

Jesus sits at the centre of a table with his twelve disciples for supper.

Jesus tells his disciples: 'Remember me with bread and wine'

Jesus and his twelve closest followers meet in an upstairs room. They have supper together, and Jesus tells them how important they will all become as teachers spreading the 'gospel', or good news, about Christian beliefs. The twelve men will become known as the Apostles, or 'messengers'.

He says a prayer, and gives each of them bread and wine. 'This is my body and blood,' he tells them. 'Whenever you eat and drink, remember my love for you and God's love for us all.'

Jesus listens to children

Jesus is often shown as a baby or a child in paintings and sculptures. St Francis (see pages 42–45) was the first to recreate the Nativity story of Jesus's simple birth in a stable at Christmas. This shows Jesus as simple and pure rather than grand or powerful.

At the age of twelve Jesus went to Jerusalem with his parents. When it was time to go home they couldn't find him. Eventually they found him at the temple talking with the priests about Moses' Law. Jesus knew that you don't have to be clever or grand to have something to say.

Years later, when his disciples tried to stop some children crowding around him, Jesus said, 'Let the children come to me, don't stop them. Heaven is for them, too.'

The Crucifixion

The Jewish leaders in Jerusalem arrested Jesus because they did not like him preaching in the temple. They brought him before the Roman Prefect, Pontius Pilate, who sentenced him to be crucified. The Romans used to put troublemakers to death by nailing them to wooden crosses. The cross has now become the most important symbol of Christianity.

The letters stand for 'Jesus Nazarenus, Rex Judaeorum' (Jesus of Nazareth, King of the Jews). The words were painted on a wooden sign that hung above Jesus's head.

MUHAMMAD

WHO WAS MUHAMMAD?

Muhammad lived **570–632**

He was also known as **Muhammad ibn 'Abdullah, Messenger of Islam, Prophet of Allah (God)** – an ancient prayer book lists 201 names for him

In which country **Arabia**

Where? **Middle East**

Religious association **Islam**

Quality **Submission:** 'Submit to one God'

Many Muslims believe that Muhammad is so holy that his face cannot be pictured. Even his name, written here in artistic writing called calligraphy, is always highly honoured.

Muhammad was a prophet who founded Islam and united the tribes of Arabia under one god. His visions of the angel Gabriel in a cave on Mount Hira above the city of Mecca are recited in the Qur'an, the sacred book of all Muslims.

'Do not let any hatred of others make you behave unfairly towards them.'
Muhammad

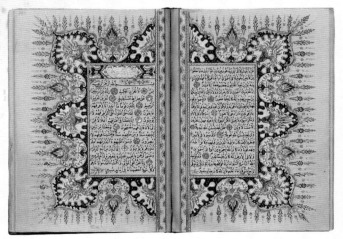

Muslims treasure these beautiful pages of the Qu'ran. They believe they contain the word of God as revealed to his Prophet Muhammad.

Muhammad enters the holy city of Mecca

Muhammad looks longingly at the sandy grey walls of the city of Mecca and prays that there will be peace today.

It has been eight years since Muhammad left the holy city and now he has returned to put an end to all the fighting between the different tribes of the region. He has led an army of 10,000 men from the city of Medina across 250 miles of the Arabian desert to ensure the safety of all those who want to worship at the sacred Ka'aba shrine in the city.

'La ilaha illa Allah!' he shouts to his men –'there is no god but God!' The army cheer and begin to advance cautiously. The leaders of Mecca have agreed to let them pass through the gates into the city.

Mecca is the city of his childhood, where his uncle had brought him up after his mother had died. It is the city where he had married his first wife, Khadija, whose camels he used to load with spices to trade in faraway cities. It is the city where he had first heard the voice of God speaking to him through the angel Gabriel in a mountain cave.

He looks up at the steep rocks which surround Mecca and his heart leaps when he sees Mount Hira, his old place of meditation. Back then, few people had wanted to listen to him when he told them to stop worshipping lots of gods and return to the one true God, and he had eventually been forced to leave Mecca and settle in Medina.

The Ka'aba is an ancient shrine in the middle of the holy city of Mecca. It is built around a black stone that is supposed to have fallen from the sky, like a meteorite, and joins heaven and earth. Whenever Muslims pray, wherever they are in the world, they turn to face this shrine.

Muslims remove their shoes and kneel to pray. Wherever they are in the world, they always face in the direction of Mecca.

Now Muhammad's message of Islam, or 'submission' to God, has attracted many followers, called 'Muslims' among the desert tribes, and he is determined to reclaim Mecca for God.

The Muslim army has now reached the holiest part of the city without any fighting. Muhammad drinks from the legendary stone well and then stands before the Ka'aba, the ancient shrine held sacred by all the different tribes and pilgrims who visit each year. Muhammad and his closest friends start to walk around the square building with great reverence, and each time they pass by its eastern corner they bend and kiss the mysterious black stone set into its walls. According to the people this stone had fallen from the sky, perhaps as a meteorite, and now represents the link between heaven and earth.

In the city of Medina in a tomb beneath a dome, Muhammad was eventually buried. Medina is the second holiest place in the world for Muslims, after Mecca.

After completing seven circuits Muhammad enters the Ka'aba, and gazes round at the many statues of different gods that the people worship here. According to legend this shrine was originally built by Abraham, the great ancestor and prophet of the people, in honour of the one true God. But for too long these idols have brought shame to the city Abraham made sacred.

He picks up one of the stone figures and hurls it to the ground. Then he smashes another, and another until they are all broken. Breathing heavily he feels as if a great weight has been lifted off his shoulders. He knows that he is the last of God's prophets, following Noah, Abraham, Moses and Jesus, and it is his duty to make sure that only the true God will be worshipped in this place. The people of Mecca and Medina must submit to the one God under one religion and unite as one people.

Outside, in the heat of the day, the Muslim soldiers from Medina kneel and bow down to God's sacred shrine. But the people of Mecca look nervously at one another, unsure of what their old enemies will do to them. Many of them fear they will be massacred. Muhammad is about to speak.

'People of Medina and Mecca,' says Muhammad to the crowds, 'from now on no tribe or people can claim to be better than another. God has put an end to such pride and ignorance, because all of us are descended from Adam. We are not separate tribes. We are one people. We do not serve different gods. We are united under the one true God.'

There is silence for a moment as this new idea takes hold among the people. Then they start to turn to one another murmuring agreement in growing relief.

Muhammad turns to the leaders of the main Meccan tribe who had fought so fiercely against his men in the past.

'And how shall I deal with you?' he asks.

A wave of tension grips the people once more as they remember the bitterness between the two sides. Someone shouts out: 'Kindly, noble prophet!' Others in the crowd repeat it until it echoes round the sacred site.

Muhammad nods.

'Then you are forgiven!' he announces. 'And all of you must now replace your bitterness with goodwill, so that where there was once hatred friendship may grow instead.'

The Hajj: in the footsteps of Muhammad

The Hajj, or pilgrimage to Mecca, is a special journey that Muslims try to make once in their lifetime to show their submission to Allah and their fellowship with other Muslims round the world. They walk around the Ka'aba, and drink from the Zamzam well.

On their way to Mecca many Muslim pilgrims gather at the Hira cave at Jabal al-Nur ('mountain of light') outside the city. It is here that Muhammad is said to have received the word of Allah (God) that is written down in the holy Muslim book, the Qu'ran.

The Qu'ran is read by Muslims all over the world today. It is written in Arabic. All but one of the chapters begin with these words:

'In the name of Allah the most merciful and the most kind…'
Qu'ran

Where is the holy city of Mecca?

The city of Mecca was Muhammad's birthplace and home for much of his life. It is the holiest place in the Islamic world, located 45 miles inland from the Red Sea port of Jeddah, Saudi Arabia.

Tradition tells us that Ishmael, son of the prophet Abraham, found the Zamzam well, and this plentiful water supply meant that Mecca became an important stopping place for traders crossing the dry desert. The well is still there today.

The ancient shrine called the Ka'aba was built in the centre of Mecca by the prophet Abraham. Every year huge crowds of people come here to walk round the Ka'aba seven times and drink from the Zamzam well, just as Muhammad did fourteen centuries ago.

The muezzin calls the faithful to prayer five times a day. He calls from a minaret (tower) above the mosque, facing towards the Ka'aba.

At the end of their long journey, pilgrims walk seven times around the Ka'aba. This photograph shows how many people are walking around the shrine to complete their Hajj – all the moving people are seen here as a blur.

ST FRANCIS

WHO WAS ST FRANCIS?

St Francis lived **1181–1226**

He was also known as **Giovanni Francesco di Bernardone, Francis of Assisi**

In which country? **Italy**

Where? **Europe**

Religious association **Christianity**

Quality **Humility:** think of others first

◀ • • • • •

Francis was born to a rich family, but he gave everything away and devoted himself to the poor. He carries a Christian cross and Bible.

St Francis tried to follow the example of Jesus by living as a poor monk, preaching with his band of friars or 'brothers'. He is considered one of the most important leaders in Christianity, who taught his followers to think about others before themselves, and to try to live like Jesus. Francis loved nature – he once said Nature was 'the mirror of God'. He is the patron saint of animals and the environment.

'It is in giving that we receive.'
St Francis

Francis begins a new and simple life

Francis is at a crossroads outside the town of Assisi (in the country we call Italy today). He has just come from the leper house where he has nursed some of the sick and now he is on his way to church. But he feels lost.

Pulling his rough coat tighter round him against the chilly morning air Francis looks wistfully up the hill towards the walls of his home town. When he was younger he used to love all the parties there and the fine clothes he used to wear. But now, at the age of 27, he no longer has any money or any friends, and he is on bad terms with his father. He has no one.

It has been three years since he saw a vision of Jesus in the small crumbling church of St Damian nearby and heard a voice telling him what to do: 'Go, Francis, and repair my house, which you see is falling into ruin.'

Francis had immediately taken some of his father's fine cloth to sell and offered the money to the priest of St Damian's, but the priest had refused it. Frightened of his father's anger Francis had run away and hidden in a cave.

◄ • • • • • •
Francis looks up to heaven and sees the hand of God reaching down. Francis has just taken off his clothes and given them to his father (the man with a golden yellow robe) to show he doesn't care about rich things or money. Behind Francis a bishop holds up a cloth to cover his naked body. The artist has painted a halo to show Francis is a saint.

43

Francis preaching to the birds. He called the birds his 'brothers and sisters' – to him, all creatures should praise God. The birds sing their praise, and Francis and his followers sang hymns as they walked barefoot in the Italian countryside.

When Francis returned to Assisi one month later, looking dirty and dejected, the townspeople mocked him and his father beat him.

Gripping a long walking stick Francis continues along the woodland track until he reaches the little chapel of St Mary of the Angels. Last year, with the help of the local stonemasons he restored its broken walls and built himself a wooden hut nearby to live in. He had already rebuilt the church of St Damian's using stones he had begged for in Assisi. But what should he do now, he wonders? Where is his life going?

Inside the simple chapel the priest and a few farming families have gathered to celebrate Mass.

'And Jesus sent out his disciples with these instructions,' the priest reads from the Bible. Francis recognizes the verse.

'Heal the sick and cleanse those with leprosy.' *Yes*, thinks Francis, *I already try to do that.*

'Do not take along any gold or silver or copper in your belts; take no bag for the journey, or extra tunic, or sandals or stick.'

A strange feeling washes over the young man. It is if Jesus is speaking directly to him. Francis is overcome with joy.

'Yes!' he cries, leaping up. 'A true disciple of Jesus gives no thought for himself. This is what I must do with all my strength.' He throws off his coat and leather belt and finds a piece of rope to tie round his coarse woollen tunic. Then he kicks off his sandals and steps outside into the fresh air. It is a beautiful spring day and the countryside is bursting with new life. He knows exactly where he is going now.

With Jesus' words of poverty and charity echoing in his mind, Francis begins to walk up the hill singing hymns and smiling. His mission will be the simple gospel of giving, and his monastery will be the open countryside and the goodwill of the people.

'God give you peace,' he says to anyone he meets on the road.

When he reaches the town square of Assisi, the people who used to scoff at him pause in wonder at his transformation.

'God loves us all,' he tells them, 'and he is ready to hear each one of us. He is ready to help us mend any wrongs we may have done. And he is ready to welcome us to his love and his peace.'

A wealthy young man called Bernard is so impressed he wonders whether he too should give away all that he has and join Francis. So do a handful of others. Today is the beginning of a new life of simplicity and hardship for Francis. And one day he and his followers will be blessed by the Pope and become the Order of Friars Minor (or 'lesser brothers').

'Where there is hatred, let me sow love.' St Francis

The church inside a church

This tiny church near Assisi was in ruins when Francis first saw it.
He rebuilt it himself and lived nearby. Here he started the Order of
Friars Minor, or Franciscans, as these monks are usually called.
The big building around it is a church that was built 350 years
after Francis died, to protect his church and to make room for
hundreds of visiting pilgrims. Today thousands of visitors come
every week.

DOGEN

WHO WAS DOGEN?

Dogen lived **1200–1253**
He was also known as **Dogen Kigen**, or **Eihei Dogen**
In which country? **Japan**
Where? **Asia**
Religious association **Zen Buddhism**
Quality **Stillness**: sitting still in meditation brings insight

◄ ·······
Dogen was a Japanese Buddhist monk. He wrote verses called Shobogenzo, 'Treasures of the Eye of True Teaching'.

Eihei Dogen was a master of 'zen', which means meditation. The type of sitting meditation ('zazen') he learned helped him to empty his mind and develop deep insight. His 'Soto' school of Zen Buddhism has many followers today.

What is this world?
Moonlight, reflected
In dewdrops,
Shaken from a bird's beak.
Dogen

Zen Buddhist artists would draw a circle (called 'enso') as a sort of special symbol. It is hollow, yet also stands for the Universe. Zen Buddhists sometimes use it to meditate.

Dogen teaches a lesson: 'How to think of nothing'

Just before dawn, when lessons begin, a boy asks his teacher Dogen about meditation. What does it mean? Is it hard?

It is four o'clock in the morning and the bell has just sounded in the Eihei-ji monastery high up in the snow-fresh mountains of Japan. Wearing rough robes Dogen, the senior monk, joins the other monks in the training hall. They greet each other silently, bowing at the waist with their hands pressed together in front of them. It is time for 'zazen', the practice of sitting meditation, where the monks stay completely still for over an hour and empty their minds. The youngest monk, a thirteen-year-old student, is finding this difficult.

'Master, how is it possible to think of nothing?' he asks Dogen.

The great Zen Master collects his thoughts. Like this young student he, too, became a Buddhist monk when he was thirteen.

'Zazen is beyond thinking of nothing,' he says. His voice is light and clear. 'If you try to think of nothing then you are still holding onto the thought you have set yourself. Zazen is losing all these intentions and decisions – about what you want and how things seem to you – until you exist only in what is real and now, thoughtless.'

Dogen built this monastery far away from Kyoto, the capital city in those days, in order to practise the true Buddhism that he had discovered in China. Dogen started a Zen Buddhist monastery for women as well as one for men.

The student shakes his head.

'What is the point of having no thoughts, Master?'

Dogen smiles. He was just the same at this age – always asking questions and never being satisfied with the answers.

'When you become still in body and mind everything becomes clear, just as a muddy puddle will slowly settle into a pure reflection. You sense your true inner nature, and the nature of everything else in the universe. You see, everything is one unity.'

Ever since Dogen had lost both parents as a child he had been trying to make sense of human life and death, and during his youth he had questioned many Zen Masters in his search for an answer. He had tried reciting Buddhist verses, but these only seemed to touch the surface. Eventually, while studying in China, he had found the ultimate peace through zazen, in the pure depths of his own human nature – free of body, free of mind – clear and true.

'I will show you,' says Dogen.

How to meditate

'Can you sit like this?' Dogen sits cross-legged on a thick mat and pulls each foot onto the opposite thigh. 'This is the lotus position. It does not matter if you cannot. Just sit comfortably. Now place your hands in your lap, one holding the other, palms upwards, with the tips of your thumbs touching. Sit up straight so that you can breathe deeply and look at the floor in front of you through half-closed eyes. Close your mouth,' Dogen says gently, 'and press your tongue against your upper palate. Now concentrate on each breath – inhaling down to your navel – and then exhaling slowly. To begin with try counting each breath, and if your mind wanders let the thought finish before starting to count from one again. Have patience and relax.'

'To study Buddhism is to study oneself.
To study oneself is to forget oneself.
To forget oneself is to be enlightened by everything.
To be enlightened by everything is to forget
all differences between things.'
Dogen

This is how to hold your hands in your lap for zazen meditation: one hand resting in the other, palms upwards, with the tips of your thumbs touching.

Dogen gently rocks back and forth until he settles into a balanced stillness. Then he breathes in deeply through his nose. Outside rain is dripping off the wide roof onto the wooden balcony. The cedar trees nearby are breathing softly. The mountain is still.

The boy copies his master. Ten minutes go by, then another ten minutes. The monks are still sitting. Their minds are clear – empty and aware. A thoughtless pulse. Reflecting nature. Inspiring. Exhaling.

As the other monks rise and leave, the young monk is left sitting. He is aware but at ease in himself. Dogen is impressed. He holds his hands to his chest and very slowly walks from the hall.

'Listen to your true inner voice and do good for others without thinking of yourself. This is the first step towards losing your own bias.'
Dogen

What is a 'koan'?

'Koan' is a Japanese word that Dogen learned in China. It is a sort of word puzzle, often in the form of a question. By meditating on this word puzzle, Dogen would try to understand a problem.

Here is a famous example:

'Two hands clap and there is a sound –
what is the sound of one hand?'

RUMI

WHO WAS RUMI?

Rumi lived **1207–73**

He was also known as **Mowlana Jalal ad-Din Muhammad Balkhi**, or just **Mowlana** (Persian for 'Master'), or **Mevlevi** (Turkish for 'Master').

In which country? Born in **Persia**, lived in **Turkey**

Where? **Middle East**

Religious association **Islam**

Quality **Love**: love for all can be felt through music and dance

◄ ······

Rumi was born in a part of Persia once ruled by the Roman Empire. The name 'Rumi' comes from the word for 'Roman', once used to describe that region.

Rumi's tomb is next to the Mosque of Selim in Konya, Central Anatolia, Turkey. Christians and Jews joined Muslims at his funeral.

Jalal ad-Din Rumi was one of the greatest Muslim poets in the Sufi tradition of Islam, which seeks a more personal, 'mystical' experience of God. Spinning round and round to music, he started a new kind of dancing meditation called the 'Sema'. He founded the Mevlevi order of 'whirling dervishes' in Konya (in modern-day Turkey).

'When we are dead, seek not our tomb in the earth, but find it in the hearts of men.'
Rumi

Rumi comes closer to God through music

The water mill goes round and round and Rumi listens to the sound of creaking wood with each turn of the wheel. 'Love is the water of life. Drink it down with heart and soul!' the famous poet sings.

Rumi often comes to sit by the water mill, a few miles outside his home town of Konya, to write poems and to remember his beloved friend Shams of Tabriz, who died a few years ago. Although Rumi learned about Islam as a boy, it was this wild Sufi mystic who first opened Rumi's heart to the love of God. 'Knowing about God is different from knowing God,' Shams told him.

When he was young Rumi had journeyed to many great cities. When he was twelve his whole family had to leave their home in Persia to escape the invasions of the Mongol armies led by Genghis Khan. They had spent some time in Baghdad as well as making the holy pilgrimage to Mecca. Today, like his father and like Shams before him, Rumi is a teacher of Islam.

Filled with the sounds of nature by the water mill, Rumi now looks up to see a caravan of travellers, chattering and laughing. They are heading along the well-worn road to Konya, carrying goods to sell on the silk and spice routes between Europe, Arabia and the Orient. Rumi decides to go to join them to hear news about the distant lands they have visited.

As the caravan approaches the city Rumi can see the Sultan's palace on top of the citadel. Leaving his newfound companions in the market place Rumi spots one of his best friends, Salah al-Din, and embraces him warmly. Rumi's son is married to Salah al-Din's daughter. Salah al-Din is a goldsmith whose apprentices are working hard in his shop, hammering pieces of gold into shape. Rumi stops and listens. The apprentices are beating out a rhythm which sounds like the repeated words 'la ilaha illa Allah!' – 'no god but God!' Rumi's face breaks into a wide smile and he begins to turn round and round with his arms wide, chanting in time with the hammering beat.

*'I always thought that
I was me – but no,
I was you
and never knew it.'*
Rumi

Who are the Dervishes?

Many Sufi Muslims seek God through the 'Sema' dance. They whirl together to the music of a drum and reed flute. 'The whirling belongs to you and you belong to the whirling,' Rumi tells them. He speaks his poetry to them, breathing God's love like a flute. His followers call him 'Mevlevi' ('Master') in Turkish, which becomes the name of his Order of dancing Sufi mystics, known as the Whirling Dervishes.

Salah al-Din is delighted and starts to twirl too. But he cannot keep up with Rumi's dizzying speed and soon he returns to the shade of his shop – 'Keep beating! Keep beating!' he calls to his workers. He can see that Rumi is lost in a trance and does not want to interrupt him.

With each spin Rumi's cloak fans out around his legs. It feels so natural to dance like this that he lets his arms and legs move as freely as if they had their own mind. He remembers that when Shams died he used to turn round and round a pole in his garden in order to lose himself in his memories, and now he feels the same closeness to everything around him.

As he spins his eyes are fixed on his left hand which points towards the earth while his right hand is raised towards the sky. In his mind his body is mirroring the rhythm of life, dancing round in a circle just as the universe dances round man. He is no longer a separate individual but feels part of a greater mind. He is enjoying the true understanding of God's perfect oneness.

He dances for what seems like hours. As the day draws to a close Rumi's whirling gets slower and slower until he comes to a gentle halt. It is dusk and he aches with happiness and love for all humanity.

Salah al-Din approaches him full of wonder at what he has just seen.

'My friend,' he says, 'I saw you dancing, but you were not there.'

'I was with God,' Rumi smiles at him. Salah al-Din frowns.

'But how is this not taught in our scriptures?'

Rumi envelops Salah al-Din in a warm gaze.

'Salah my good friend, it seems there are many places to look for understanding. Christian, Jew, Muslim, stone, mountain, river – each has a secret way of being with the mystery, unique and not to be judged.'

The two friends part, knowing that something very special has brought them closer together. And Rumi starts to think that he will have something different and wonderful to tell his students tomorrow morning.

'To love is to reach God.'
Rumi

◄ • • • • •
Whirling Dervishes dance to the sound of drums and reed flutes.

JOAN OF ARC

WHO WAS SAINT JOAN?

Joan of Arc lived **1412–1431**

She was also known as the **Maid of Orléans**, **Jehanne La Pucelle** (Joan the maid), **Jeanne d'Arc**. The name 'd'Arc' is her surname.

In which country? **France**

Where? **Europe**

Religious association **Christianity**

Quality **Inspiration**: strong belief triumphs

Joan was a peasant girl who led the French troops into battle, mounted on horseback and carrying a banner that reads 'In the name of God'.

Joan of Arc led the French Army to victory at the age of seventeen. As an ordinary peasant girl she persuaded the Dauphin (heir to the throne) of France, Charles VII, that she heard the voices of angels and saints telling her to save France, and her strength of belief inspired all who saw her. The Dauphin sent her to lead his troops into battle.

Joan preferred to be known as Jehanne la Pucelle (in English 'Joan the maid'). The king is said to have designed her coat of arms with a crown, a sword and two fleur-de-lis ('lily flowers' – the French royal symbol).

54

Joan kneels before the Dauphin. As a French military leader, she inspired his troops to drive the English out of the city of Reims. Later Joan stood next to the Dauphin as he was crowned King Charles VII of France.

The fate of France rests in the hands of a seventeen-year-old girl

In the royal castle of Chinon, Joan stands in the middle of the Great Hall. Her dark hair is cut short and and she is dressed in men's clothes. There is something about her that makes the gathered company uneasy. They are noble and grand and important, and she is just an ordinary girl from the faraway village of Domrémy. Yet she shows no trace of fear.

Joan has insisted that she speak to the Dauphin, soon to be King Charles VII of France. He is dressed as a nobleman and stands among all the lords and bishops to see if she will know which one he is. Her eyes dart from face to face. She has never seen the heir to the throne before, nor even a picture of him.

She stops in front of a tall young man – she has found him.

'Noble Dauphin,' she says, bowing low. 'I am Joan. I have come in the name of God to lead you to the town of Reims where you will be crowned King.'

The assembled dignitaries know that Reims is occupied by allies of the English in Northern France.

'Who has sent you?' the Dauphin asks. He has heard the rumours about Joan hearing voices.

'When I was twelve,' she replies, 'as I was tending my father's sheep I saw a beautiful light, which spoke to me. He said he was the Archangel Michael –'

There is laughter in the Great Hall.

'– and later I heard Saint Catherine and Saint Margaret speaking to me too,' Joan insists. She holds the Dauphin's gaze.

'They told me to drive out the English, and to crown the rightful king of France.' There is silence at Joan's continued boldness.

'And when people doubt me,' she looks around at all the faces watching her, 'I pray to God. And each time I hear a voice that says: "Daughter of God, go, go, go. I will help you. Go." And I am filled with great joy.'

The Dauphin is impressed. But he is uneasy about such a young girl claiming to speak to God. Is this allowed by the Church? Could she be a witch? Might she claim to speak with a higher authority than him?

The Dauphin decides to send Joan to the nearby town of Poitiers to be tested by the top bishops and experts. But they can find nothing wrong with her answers. She seems a perfect example of piety and self-belief, although on occasions she is quite impatient with their questions.

At last the Dauphin agrees to let her lead his army. He is desperate. The English are besieging the town of Orléans further up the river Loire and the French troops are demoralized. Maybe this simple girl will bring God's inspiration to the next battle, he prays. If not, he is in danger of losing the rest of his kingdom.

Joan leads the French into battle at Orléans

A knight's squire helps Joan put on her suit of armour. Then he hoists her high onto a white horse and hands her a flowing banner.

Bright and gleaming for all to see, Joan leads 4,000 French soldiers towards Orléans accompanied by several priests singing hymns in Latin. She has made every soldier go to church regularly.

When they reach Orléans Joan writes to the English Commander, Lord Talbot, demanding that he withdraw his army immediately. But a few days later the French commanders begin an attack on the English without telling her. Angry but determined she rides out through the cannon-fire and smoke to join her soldiers, waving her banner and shouting encouragement.

Joan sees that they are trying to raise ladders against a tower overlooking the bridge, and she dismounts to help them. An English arrow thuds into her shoulder, knocking her to the ground. She can hardly breathe with the pain. Soldiers carry her away so that her wound can be treated. But when she hears that the attack is being halted she mounts her horse again and charges back into the fray.

'In God's name, forward boldly!' she cries.

The men are amazed to see her banner. They rally to her call, sensing that God must be with them. With renewed strength they beat back the shaken English until the enemy is overcome and the city is at last free.

When news of the victory reaches the Dauphin he knows that this small peasant girl has just turned the course of history.

Joan of Arc shows her troops the way to victory. Some of the defenders cannot believe that a woman is leading the attack – and she is so young. But Joan is fearless, because she believes that God has given her courage. Soon she will be captured, however, and her faith will be tested.

Joan of Arc was taken to this tower in the city of Rouen, France. It is still there today.

Why was Joan put to death?

After leading the French to many more victories, Joan was captured and imprisoned. The English threatened her with torture in this tower.

Joan was put on trial for heresy (disagreeing with religious leaders). Some said she was a witch. The judges tried to trick her into admitting she was guilty, but she wasn't fooled. Finally she was condemned to burn to death. Her last words were 'Jesus, Jesus'.

Twenty years later the Church leaders said she had been wrongly put to death.

In 1920, nearly 500 years after she died, Joan was declared a saint.

GURU NANAK

WHO WAS GURU NANAK?

Guru Nanak lived **1469–1539**
He was also known as **Nanak Dev**
In which country? **India**
Where? **Asia**
Religious association **Sikhism**
Quality **Devotion**: inner devotion brings equality before God

Guru Nanak as an old man, with his prayer beads ••••••▶

Guru Nanak was the founder of the Sikh religion in northwest India (now Pakistan). He rejected the class divisions and religious differences of his time and taught an inner devotion to god without display or ritual.

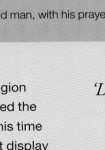

'Love god as a fish loves water.' Guru Nanak

Guru Nanak as a young man, discussing ideas with Hindu holy men. The man behind him is keeping flies away from him.

Nanak celebrates his thread ceremony

Everyone is excited. The day has arrived for Nanak's sacred thread ceremony, when his family celebrate the day he is considered a full member of the community. He is sitting in the shaded courtyard of his house. The priest has arrived to place a special sacred thread over his shoulder. Everyone is making a fuss, but Nanak thinks: What is the point?

Nanak's father, Talwandi, catches his eye and nods at him reassuringly. He is an important man in their village because he works as the bookkeeper for the local Muslim landlord.

Pandit Hardial, the family priest, begins to recite a passage from the Vedas, the oldest of the Hindu scriptures. Nanak recognizes the verse. He knows a lot about Hindu theology, sometimes even more than his teacher at school, he thinks. But what is the need for all this stuffy ritual? He would much rather be out in the fields, thinking about God and making up his own hymns.

The Pandit holds up the sacred thread with great reverence. (It's just a piece of string, thinks Nanak.) With a flourish the holy man places the woven strands on the boy's left shoulder. The three twisted strands of cotton signify purity of thought, word, and deed. Nanak shakes his head and lifts the thread off his shoulder.

'Dear Pandit, I don't see the point of this,' he says. There is a stir among the assembled guests. The priest pauses for a moment.

'My boy,' he explains, 'without this thread you will only belong to the lowest class of people in this country. By putting it on you attain greatness of spirit. You become twice-born.'

'Surely not, dear Pandit,' Nanak replies, amid more uncomfortable murmurs around him. He does not mean to be rude but he feels he cannot let this go. 'By wearing this thread I am the same person I have always been. It has no effect on my soul. If the thread were made of happiness, or if it gave me knowledge, then it would be a real gift to wear.'

'Listen to me, Nanak,' the priest fixes his eyes on him. 'This tradition goes back for centuries. And you are only a boy. Do you think that we, your elders, know nothing? By refusing this thread you show yourself to be without religion.'

'But it doesn't show anything,' Nanak insists. 'You can wear it and still lie and cheat and steal. Devotion to God is the one true unbreakable thread which the soul can wear, not all this ritual.' Nanak is aware that his father is glaring at him.

'I'm sorry,' he says, 'but I just know that in the eyes of God all humans are equal. No one can say that one group is better than another just because of his birth or because of a thread ceremony. Or even because he is a man.' He points to his sister who is standing with their mother. 'Why is Bibi not allowed to wear the sacred thread? Is it because she is a girl?'

When they are old enough, young Hindu boys take part in a special ceremony where they are given a sacred thread to wear for the rest of their life.

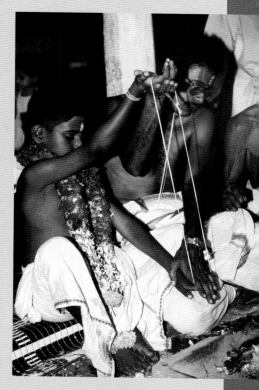

The Sikh holy book Adi Granth contains all Guru Nanak's teachings. The tenth Guru (or teacher) declared that he was to be followed not by another teacher, but by this book instead. Since then the holy scripture has also been called Guru Granth Sahib.

The Pandit is at a loss what to say or do. Although most of the guests are shocked by Nanak's impertinence, some people think to themselves: maybe Nanak is right.

Nanak is on the path to becoming a teacher, or 'guru'. And he will soon have followers, or 'sikhs', who want to devote themselves to an idea of god that is not spoiled by the traditions of either Hinduism or Islam. One day he will travel throughout India and to Arabia, too, calling people back to a god without meaningless ritual or diversions. He will speak out against all divisions of caste, religion and gender. And he will name a guru to take his place after he is gone.

'Love the saints of every faith:
Put away your pride.
Remember the essence of religion
Is meekness and sympathy.'
Guru Nanak

People join a huge crowd to visit the Sikh holy book, Guru Granth Sahib, at the Golden Temple in Amritsar, Punjab, India. •••••➤

MARTIN LUTHER

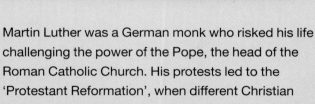

WHO WAS MARTIN LUTHER?

Martin Luther lived **1483–1546**

In which country? **Germany**

Where? **Europe**

Religious association **Christianity**

Quality **Integrity**: being completely honest, sticking to your beliefs

Martin Luther wearing his monk's robes. When he was a young man, Luther was almost struck by a lightning bolt. He then told his father that from that day he had vowed to become a monk.

Martin Luther was a German monk who risked his life challenging the power of the Pope, the head of the Roman Catholic Church. His protests led to the 'Protestant Reformation', when different Christian churches decided not to follow the Pope's orders.

'Truth is everlasting, but our ideas about truth are changeable.'

Martin Luther

Luther writes his words on a door with a huge pen. In real life, he actually nailed a piece of paper to the door of a church in Wittenberg.

Martin Luther is shown on the right, preaching from a bible. His words go up to heaven, through a holy lamb (an ancient symbol), then through Jesus Christ (shown kneeling), straight to God, who is dressed as a king. The words are not in Latin, they are in German – which all the people shown in this picture can understand.

Martin Luther tells the Emperor: 'the Pope is wrong'

Martin Luther gets ready to stand up in front of the Emperor and repeat his protest against the Pope. He could be put to death for saying it.

'Oh God!' he begs, 'Help me, please! Everything is against me.'

The thirty-eight-year-old monk is alone in a lodging house in the small town of Worms (in modern-day Germany). He will soon have to face the Grand Assembly (called the 'Diet') of the Holy Roman Empire to defend his accusations against the Pope.

More than three years ago, in 1517, Martin Luther wrote a list of ninety-five 'theses' (or arguments) against the corruption of the Catholic Church and nailed them to the church door in the town of Wittenberg, where he teaches at the university. When he refused to withdraw what he had written, the Pope told him he had to leave the Church.

The Emperor (on his throne, in the centre) waits to hear what Luther has to say. Will he still make accusations against the Pope?

Although the Emperor has promised to protect him, Luther remembers what happened to John Hus, who disagreed with the Pope one hundred years before. Hus was promised safety too, but then he was burned to death.

'How can I defend the truth against those who want to burn me?' Luther prays. The troubled monk begins to read the Bible in order to prepare what he has to say. The Roman Catholic Church could be changed forever, and Martin Luther's life could be in danger.

There is a knock at the door. It is an officer: 'I have come to escort you to the Diet,' he says. Luther knows the time has come to say what he believes.

The people of Worms jostle in the streets to see the man who dares to challenge the Pope's authority. Many have even climbed onto the roofs of houses to get a better look at him. At the door to the town hall a white-haired army general puts a hand on Luther's shoulder. 'Poor monk,' he says, 'you are about to make a nobler stand than any of my soldiers in battle. If you are sure you are right then you have nothing to fear. God be with you.'

Martin Luther's thin face is pale, and he looks ill. But there is now a new fire behind his eyes. Yesterday the Diet asked him to take back his criticisms of the Pope. Today he will give his answer – and his life will depend on it.

The officer leads him into a large room crowded with German princes and dukes, and sets him in front of the throne of Charles V, ruler over much of Europe. Immediately the Archbishop's assistant, Doctor Eck, rises and points sternly to a pile of books on a table.

'How do you defend your writings?' he asks sternly.

Martin Luther takes a deep breath and, facing the Emperor, he says:

'Most Serene Emperor, I have challenged the Pope for claiming things

Pope Leo X (shown in the middle) was the most powerful man in the Christian Church, with headquarters in Rome. He raised large sums of money to spend on building churches.

that are not in the Bible. He says that a sinner can buy forgiveness from a priest with an indulgence – money, so that his soul can get into heaven more quickly when he dies. But forgiveness is a gift of God. It comes from within, from sincere repentance.'

The assembled nobles listen closely. They know that the Pope needs to raise money to build St Peter's, his grand, expensive new church in Rome.

'The Pope has no power to forgive sins and neither do his priests. It is against the teachings of Scripture,' Luther says in a firm voice, 'and the Pope is not above Scripture.'

Dr Eck stamps on the bare floorboards in anger. 'Will you take back your accusations? Yes or no?'

Martin Luther looks round at all the powerful men gathered in the hall. 'If anyone here can give me evidence from the Bible that shows I am wrong,' he says, 'I will happily burn these books myself.' A year ago the Pope's supporters in Rome made a great display of burning copies of Martin Luther's books, so he in turn burnt the Pope's official letter (called a 'papal bull') condemning his teachings.

'If I take back what I have written,' Luther continues, 'it would only strengthen the tyranny of Rome over the faithful of Europe. My lords, I cannot act against my conscience, so I cannot take back what I have written. Here I stand; I can do no other. May God help me. Amen.'

CHIEF SEATTLE

WHO WAS CHIEF SEATTLE?

Chief Seattle lived **1786–1866**.
He is also known as **Si'ahl** or **Sealth** – these are spellings that try to show the right way to say his name in his language.
In which country? **USA**
Where? **North America**
Religious association **Traditional Native American beliefs**
Quality **Harmony**: love one another in harmony with nature

This is the only known photograph of Chief Seattle ......▶

Chief Seattle made a famous speech urging the white settlers in his homeland to live in harmony with nature. As the leader of the Suquamish and Duwamish tribes in what is now Washington State in America, he spoke for all Native Americans about the important link between the people's spirit and their environment.

'*Treat the earth well –*
It was not given to you by your parents,
It was loaned to you by your children.
We do not inherit the earth from
our ancestors –
We borrow it from our children.'
Native American proverb

Chief Seattle makes a speech to the new arrivals

Chief Seattle stands above the bay, breathing in the clean morning air. It has been many summers since he first saw the white people come. Now they are here again on the beach. They have come to take the land of his people, the land of his ancestors. He must speak with them, for he is no longer a warrior to fight them.

Chief Seattle is old, but still tall and broad, and his face is proud. Behind him is his tepee, a large tent wrapped in the buffalo skins he hunted for in his youth. Like an Emperor stepping down from his throne Chief Seattle slowly descends the grass slope. His granddaughter walks with him.

'Before our white brothers arrived,' he says, 'to make us civilized people, we had no prison, no locks nor keys, and no money to measure ourselves by. And now they want us to live in square boxes in cities where there is no quiet place. And they want us to live by their holy book.' He shakes his head and bends closer to the young girl. 'They do not know that if you open a book to the wind and the rain, soon the words will be gone. Our bible *is* the wind.'

The blue water in the bay below swarms with canoes and the shore is lined with people from the Suquamish and Duwamish tribes. The Governor of the white man's new territory, Isaac Stevens, has arrived. He is a short man with a neat beard, and he is smartly dressed in a dark coat and silk scarf.

Governor Isaac Stevens (seated) and some of his officers. He was a soldier who was made first Governor of Washington Territory.

Only 40 years after Chief Seattle's speech, the city that was named after him had begun to grow very big.

▲ Mount Rainier, in today's Washington State, was called Mount Tacoma by Native Americans. It was later renamed after Peter Rainier, a British naval officer.

With Governor Stevens is 'Doc' Maynard, the doctor who has become Chief Seattle's friend over the last few years. Doc Maynard introduces Governor Stevens, who speaks to the gathered crowd. He talks of building a railroad and urges all the different tribes of the Washington territory to give up their lands.

Chief Seattle listens. He looks across the pine forests and up to the snow-white peak of Mount Tacoma, the 'mother of waters'. Then he speaks.

'Every part of this country is sacred to my people.'
Chief Seattle

EARTH MOTHER

Chief Seattle's deep-toned voice echoes across the harbour:

'The President in Washington says he wants to buy our land. But how can you buy or sell the freshness of the air? Or the sparkle of the water? This we know: the earth does not belong to man. Man belongs to the earth. We are part of the earth, and it is part of us. The perfumed flowers are our sisters. The bear, the deer, the great eagle, these are our brothers. The streams and rivers murmur with the voice of our fathers. The wind that gave our ancestors their first breath also received their last sigh. Every part of the earth is sacred to my people. We love this earth as a newborn loves its mother's heartbeat.'

The city of Seattle today. Chief Seattle, the man the city is named after, would certainly not recognize what was once his land.

Chief Seattle turns his gaze to Governor Stevens, Doc Maynard and the other officers.

'So, white men, will you teach your children what we have taught our children? That what befalls the earth befalls all the sons of the earth? That all things are connected like the blood that unites us all? That we are all different coloured flowers of one meadow?'

Chief Seattle looks around him at all the people's faces. His eyes sparkle with the intelligent spirit behind them.

'All people share a oneness with the spirit of the universe. And all people share a oneness with each other. For the spirit of the universe lives within each one of us. And this one spirit is the peace between people and nations.'

He lifts his head to catch the sea air. But he can also smell gunpowder. And steel, brick and wire. A nation lost. He closes his eyes.

THE NATIVE INDIAN CODE

Respect nature and the balance in all things.
Respect yourself as part of nature's balance.
Respect others – their feelings, their
  differences and their freedom.
Serve others – offer kindness, generosity
  and goodwill.
Be truthful and follow what you know
  to be right.

'I give thanks for my life spirit and for the gifts of nature, and I give thanks for another day to grow in spirit and serve my people.'
Chief Seattle

BAHA'U'LLAH

WHO WAS BAHA'U'LLAH?

Baha'u'llah lived **1817–1892**
As a young man he was known as **Mirza Husayn Ali Nuri**.
   He changed his name to **Baha'u'llah**, which means
   'Splendour of God'
In which country? **Persia**
Where? **Middle East**
Religious association **Baha'i**
Quality **Unity**: world peace can be achieved through
   religious unity

Pictures of Baha'u'llah are considered by his followers to be sacred and not
to be shown in public. This is the passport he carried on his travels.

*'So powerful is the light of unity that it can
illuminate the whole earth.'* Baha'u'llah

Baha'u'llah is commemorated at the Mansion of Bahji,
once his summer house just outside Acre (Akka) in today's
northern Israel. Today it is the Baha'is most holy shrine.

Baha'u'llah came from a noble Persian family.
He became a follower of the preacher called the
Bab. The Bab said a 'Promised One' would
become the messenger of all religions. For a while
Baha'u'llah lived as a hermit. Then he claimed he
was the messenger.

Baha'u'llah set off by boat across the River Tigris to the garden of Ridvan, Baghdad, where he revealed his identity to his followers.

Baha'u'llah meets his followers on the other side of the River Tigris, where he will make an announcement

For ten years, Baha'u'llah has kept an important secret. Now, seeing his crowd of followers, the time has come to reveal his true identity.

Baha'u'llah has been banished from the city of Baghdad by the government, and people of every kind, rich and poor, young and old, are very upset and angry. He promises he will speak to them all in the garden across the water.

Baha'u'llah has a commanding presence in his tall taj hat, long black beard and dark cloak. Behind his intense eyes, a calm thrill burns, making everyone want to know what he will say to them.

It has been a long spiritual journey for Baha'u'llah to reach this point. He and his younger brother were devout Muslims, but they became keen followers of a spiritual preacher, called the Bab, meaning 'gateway to truth'.

The Bab preached that God was about to reveal another great prophet. Muslims were outraged by this claim because they believed that Muhammad was God's final prophet. The Bab was executed and Baha'u'llah was thrown into an underground dungeon, called the Black Pit. Here Baha'u'llah saw a vision of a maiden, who told him of his divine mission. It became clear to Baha'u'llah that he was actually the messenger, the one foretold by the Bab.

Now, many years later, Baha'u'llah will reveal his identity to his faithful followers. The garden is ready. There are tents for his followers among the lush trees and bright red rosebeds. Streams of water flow down from the hill. Baha'u'llah calls the garden 'Ridvan', which means Paradise.

As the setting sun casts a yellow glow over the garden Baha'u'llah calls his eldest son Abdu'l-Baha into his tent. After a short while, he calls four of his closest friends to join them. 'I have something to reveal to you,' Baha'u'llah begins. The men seated in the tent feel the importance of the occasion.

Baha'u'llah's eldest son Abdu'l-Baha was the first person to hear his father's secret. After his father died Abdu'l-Baha became the leader of the Baha'is.

71

'The Bab spoke of the one to be revealed by God, a new prophet for this age,' Baha'u'llah gazes at his friends intently, 'and I have known for some time now that God has revealed himself in me.

'I am his messenger, the one foretold by the Bab. For there is only one God, one religion, one humanity. I am the fulfilment of all the religions. I am the "Splendour of God", Baha'u'llah.'

Baha'u'llah was imprisoned in this fort in Acre (called Akka in Arabic), where many other followers of the preacher Bab were also tortured and killed.

72

'The earth is but one country and mankind its citizens.'
Baha'u'llah

Baha'u'llah spent years of his life in prison

Baha'u'llah was a spiritual leader who suffered for his religious beliefs. Shortly after the death of the famous preacher called the Bab, Baha'u'llah was accused of trying to assassinate the Shah, the ruler of Persia. He was held in the stocks for three days and given no food. Along with other prisoners, he chanted prayers so that the Shah would hear them. Later Baha'u'llah was jailed underground, in the old reservoir for the public bath. Here in the Black Pit he had his vision, which revealed his mission in life: to be the messenger of God.

After he had been released from prison, Baha'u'llah's influence grew, which made his followers, including his brother Azal, jealous and angry. Azal claimed he, not Baha'u'llah, was the messenger of God. Later Azal even tried to poison him.

Baha'u'llah spent much of his life in exile, since the ruling religious leaders worried that he was becoming too powerful and so kept him away. His final years were spent in Syria, in another prison, visited by pilgrims. Eventually he was released and died in Bahji, near Acre, in 1892.

What did Baha'u'llah believe?

Baha'u'llah believed that God revealed his teachings through messengers, including Abraham, Krishna, Zoroaster, Moses, Buddha, Jesus and Muhammad, and he said their religions come from the same God. Baha'u'llah believed himself to be the latest of these messengers. His faith centres on an essential message of unity, the oneness of God and the oneness of religion.

Today, members of the Baha'i faith live across the world. This temple in New Delhi is based on the shape of a lotus flower opening to the sky, like the flowers in the garden of Ridvan.

WHAT DID BAHA'U'LLAH WRITE?

Baha'u'llah wrote important religious books and taught the importance of following a spiritual path. One, *The Seven Valleys*, answers questions he was asked by a religious group called the Sufis, whom he had met when he was a hermit. Baha'u'llah was also a keen letter writer. While in exile in Syria he wrote to Queen Victoria, Napoleon III, Tsar Alexander II of Russia and Pope Pius IX to spread the word of his faith.

GANDHI

WHO WAS GANDHI?

Gandhi lived **1869–1948**

His birth name was **Mohandas Karamchand Gandhi**, but he came to be called **Mahatma** ('great soul')

In which country? **India**

Where? **Asia**

Religious association **Hinduism**

Quality **Satyagraha** (peaceful resistance): truth and justice can be achieved through peaceful resistance

◀••••••

Mohandas Karamchand Gandhi, called Mahatma. Gandhi's birthday, 2 October, has been chosen by the United Nations as an International Day of Non-Violence

Mahatma Gandhi was called the 'Father of the Nation' of India. As a young man he was a lawyer in South Africa where he encouraged *satyagraha*, non-violent resistance against unfairness and injustice. He went on to lead India to self-rule, instead of continuing under the rule of the British Empire.

'*We need to be the change we wish to see in the world.*'
Gandhi

◀••••••

Gandhi's handwriting here reads 'I want world sympathy in this battle of Right against Might.' He has signed his name – 'M.K. Gandhi' – and the place and date: Dandi 5 April 1930.

The Indian flag has a wheel at its centre. In Gandhi's first design, it was a spinning wheel. By law today the flag must be made of khadi, a hand-spun cloth of the kind Gandhi used to spin himself.

Gandhi picks up salt – and breaks the law

The man they call 'Mahatma' Gandhi is on his way to the seaside. He has walked 240 miles and he can see the deep blue water on the horizon. Behind him, thousands of people follow in a long line stretching back into the distance.

Some followers have been with him ever since they set off from their ashram 23 days ago. Others have joined along the route. Ahead, crowds of people are running out of their villages to see him. They bring fresh flowers and green leaves to lay down on the dusty road. A newspaper reporter is trying to get closer. Gandhi sees him and beckons: 'What is it you want to ask me, friend?'

Gandhi is 61 years old and completely bald. He has a moustache and glasses and wears a white shawl and sandals. He walks with a long bamboo stick. The reporter falls into step beside him.

'Sir, why are all these people following you? Where are you going?'

'I am going to collect salt,' Gandhi replies with a mischievous twinkle in his eye, 'natural salt left on the beach from seawater.'

The two men know that this is against the law. For nearly 200 years India has been part of the British Empire. The British rulers want to make money from selling salt and taxing it.

'My friends and I,' Gandhi gestures behind him, 'are making a little protest. I have written a letter to the British explaining why they are wrong to make the poorest people pay for such an important part of their food when it is freely given by nature. So we are going to disobey the law and encourage all the people of India to do the same. This is our country. And it is time the British let us decide our own laws.'

By the side of the road, someone is waving the new flag of India.

'You see the spinning wheel in the middle of the flag? That is the sign of freedom for ordinary Indians. Instead of buying British clothes we weave them ourselves on spinning wheels.'

'We will fight for our freedom – not with violence and killing but with *satyagraha*, the force of truth and non-violence. I know its power from my days in South Africa.'

The beach is now in sight and all around them crowds of people are walking across the fields down to the shore.

'You are a Muslim, aren't you?' Gandhi asks the reporter. 'I have read your holy book, and the Christian book too. And although I am a Hindu I am a Muslim too – and a Christian and a Jew and a Buddhist. No religion is better than the other. What matters in the world is truth and kindness and the courage to stand up for fairness without hurting anyone. Please write that in your newspaper.'

Gandhi picks up natural salt from near the sea shore at Dandi, Gujarat, India on the morning of 6 April 1930. He is breaking the law on purpose, to show his peaceful protest against a law he thinks is deeply unfair.

'My religion is based on truth and non-violence.'
Gandhi

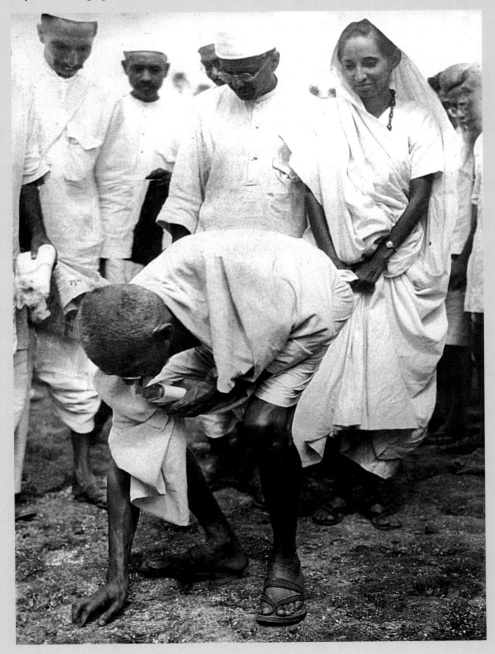

How do you change people's minds peacefully?

When Gandhi was a young lawyer in South Africa he was thrown off a train because he was Indian. He was very upset. So he started to help other Indians to be treated more fairly. He told them how to make a stand against injustice: stop working and disobey the law without fighting, even if you are attacked. As more and more people supported his moral courage the authorities were soon forced to change their minds. Peaceful bravery won against violence. That is the power of *satyagraha* (non-violent resistance).

The Raj Ghat in Delhi, India, is a shrine to the memory of Gandhi. He was shot by an assassin when he was an old man. Sadly not everyone agreed with his non-violent way of life.

'Religions are different roads converging to the same point.'
Gandhi

HAILE SELASSIE

WHO WAS HAILE SELASSIE?

Haile Selassie lived **1892–1975**

He was also known as **Tafari Makonnen, Ras Tafari, His Imperial Majesty Haile Selassie I, King of Kings, Lord of Lords, Conquering Lion of the Tribe of Judah,** and **Elect of God**

In which country? **Ethiopia**

Where? **Africa**

Religious association **Christianity, Rastafarianism**

Quality **Hope:** for freedom and unity

Haile Selassie was Emperor of Ethiopia. His followers believe he was sent by God. Haile Selassie was a Christian.

Haile Selassie is believed by Rastafarians (literally, followers of Ras Tafari, one of his names) to have been the reincarnation of Jesus, the Christian Messiah. According to legend Haile Selassie was descended directly from King Solomon and the Queen of Sheba. He became a symbol of hope for black unity in Africa and beyond, and spoke up for international cooperation and security.

'Nations and peoples can and will work together… in the assurance of that equality and brotherhood which we desire'
Haile Selassie

Haile Selassie visits the descendants of African slaves

There is great excitement at Kingston airport in Jamaica. Over 100,000 of his followers – Rastafarians – have come to see their Messiah, whose aeroplane is expected to land shortly. Some are waving palm leaves, some Ethiopian flags, and others are blowing cowhorns or beating drums.

The air is thick with expectation and the smell of cannabis smoke. Many are smoking chalice pipes filled with their 'wisdom weed', which Rastafarians use to heighten their religious experience. They look to the sky for the first glimpse of the plane but falling rain fills their eyes.

Rainwater drips from the long dreadlocks and beards worn by the Rastafarian men, and children with wet faces smile gleefully at being given a day off school. Puddles have formed around the line of guards waiting on the tarmac. Suddenly there is a cheer. An aeroplane has been spotted. And it is no longer raining. 'See how God stops the rain!' they shout.

'Apart from the Kingdom of the Lord there is not on this earth any nation that is superior to any other.'
Haile Selassie

79

People from all over Jamaica have climbed up onto the roof to get a better view of Haile Selassie, their god-like leader. The green, yellow and red of the Ethiopian flag can be seen everywhere.

The roar of the crowd is deafening as the plane comes to a halt in front of the waiting dignitaries. The people surge forward, breaking down the barriers and pushing through the lines of soldiers and police. They surround the plane chanting and holding up framed photographs of their Saviour. The pride of Africa has come to them.

The steps up to the plane are in place. The crowd are in a frenzy. Eventually the door opens and the Emperor stands for all to see. The roar of the mob is like an explosion of thunder. 'God is here!' they shout. Haile Selassie raises his hand and the noise intensifies. The Lion of Judah is a small man with a neat beard and he wears a beige military uniform with a peaked hat and a leather belt. There are tears in his eyes.

Then he disappears inside the plane again. A Rastafarian leader is found and given permission to mount the steps. He is Mortimer Planno who met the Emperor five years ago in Addis Ababa, Ethiopia's capital. Inside the plane he bows to the Emperor.

'I know you,' Haile Selassie says, addressing him in English. 'You were the one who gave me a scarf when you visited my country. You wove it yourself.'

Mortimer Planno beams with delight that Haile Selassie, the new Messiah, should remember his humble gift.

'This is quite a welcome,' Haile Selassie says, looking at the crowd outside.

A servant asks Mortimer Planno: 'His Imperial Majesty would like to know when it might be safe for him to leave the plane.'

Mortimer Planno nods excitedly and goes to the plane door.

'Be calm! Be calm!' he calls to the crowd. 'Step back and let the Emperor come.'

A few minutes later the people's Messiah is finally escorted from the plane by the police and Jamaican officials amid cheers and music.

•••••➤

The lion is the symbol of the Israelite Tribe of Judah, also adopted by Haile Selassie who was called the 'Conquering Lion of Judah'. Haile Selassie gave several lions away as imperial gifts. The colours of the Ethiopian flag have a meaning: green for the land, gold for peace and harmony, and red for African bloodshed and strength.

Slaves no more: the Emperor gives hope

Three hundred years ago, thousands of Africans were brought to Jamaica to work as slaves on the sugar plantations. Their descendants endured many hardships away from their homeland.

Marcus Garvey, a black Jamaican, told them that all black people shared the same African identity and pride. 'Look to Africa,' he said, 'when a black king shall be crowned, for the day of deliverance is at hand!'

A few years later, Haile Selassie was crowned Emperor of Ethiopia, the only African country not ruled by colonial Europeans. Far from Africa, Jamaicans rejoiced too.

◄┄┄┄┄┄

Emperor Haile Selassie stands in front of his throne on the day of his coronation.

Rastafarians and reggae

Jamaican Rastafarians are famous for their love of reggae music. Reggae singers often praise Haile Selassie, whom they call the 'new Messiah', the son of God as prophesied in the Bible in the Book of Revelations. They often wear the colours of the Ethiopian flag to show their connection with Africa.

'*We must become members of a new race, overcoming petty prejudice, owing our ultimate allegiance not to nations but to our fellow men within the human community*'
Haile Selassie

MOTHER TERESA

WHO WAS MOTHER TERESA?

Mother Teresa lived **1910–1997**

She was also known as **Agnesë Gonxhe Bojaxhiu** (her birth name). She is called **Blessed Teresa of Calcutta** by the Catholic church

In which country? Born in **Albania**, Europe, she became an **Indian** citizen

Religious association **Christianity**

Quality **Kindness**: even the very poorest deserve loving kindness

◄······

Mother Teresa spent her life working for people who were poor and dying. She was awarded the Nobel Peace Prize in 1979.

Mother Teresa cared for the poor and dying of Kolkata (Calcutta) in India. She became the most famous example of charity in the world. Born to Albanian parents, Agnes Bojaxhiu changed her name when she became a nun. She went on to set up hundreds of hospices and shelters in many different countries to help the poor and sick.

'The fruit of prayer is faith,
the fruit of faith is love,
the fruit of love is service,
the fruit of service is peace.'
Mother Teresa

'The poor must know that we love them.'
Mother Teresa

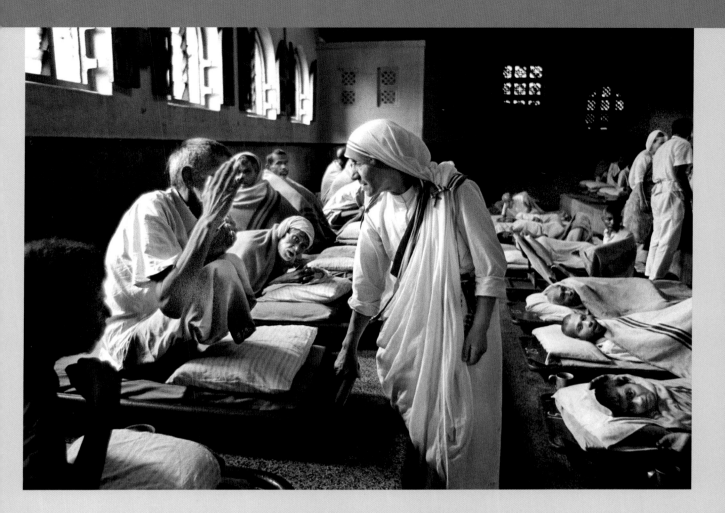

A visitor describes meeting Mother Teresa at her home for the dying

'The streets of Kolkata bustle with people and traffic and the air is hot with diesel fumes. I receive a kind welcome from the nuns at the House of the Destitute and Dying. This was the first shelter opened by Mother Teresa where the sick and abandoned are cared for with dignity.'

A long room is full of beds occupied by people with withered limbs and desperate eyes. As I watch the nuns, or 'sisters', go about their work kindly and calmly, I wonder again what inspires them to devote themselves to a lifetime of looking after the poor and the sick?

There are thousands more sisters like them working in the many other hospices and shelters all over the world. Mother Teresa is a tiny woman who has been tireless in persuading governments to help her.

I get on the bus with some of the sisters who are going out to the slums. A small elderly nun is loading boxes on to the bus. We set off through the busy streets – rickshaw pullers shout, and horns blare. It is dark by the time we arrive at an enormous rubbish dump. The stench hits us as we all get out. The small, elderly nun who I saw before takes my hand. She is dressed in a simple white sari with a blue border. Then I realize it is her – Mother Teresa.

Mother Teresa walks among the people at her home for the poor and dying in Kolkata (Calcutta). She believed every one is equal in God's eyes, and all deserve to be treated with dignity and respect.

'You have been sent by God,' Mother Teresa says, and she smiles up at me.

I feel overwhelmed. Here is the most famous woman in the world, among the flies and squalor of this appalling place, and she is holding my hand. I am mesmerized by the kindness and energy in her wrinkled face.

We find a woman lying in some mud. It seems she has been lying there for days. Mother Teresa kneels down next to her. The woman has a burning fever and her feet have been half eaten away by rats and ants.

'My son has abandoned me,' she murmurs.

'You must forgive your son,' Mother Teresa urges. 'He regrets abandoning you. Be a mother to him and forgive him.'

The woman starts to weep. 'I forgive him,' she says eventually, in a quiet voice. And then her face lights up with a beautiful smile.

'Thank you,' she whispers, and she closes her eyes.

Mother Teresa takes my arm and leads me away. For someone so tiny she is surprisingly strong and she walks quickly too. She turns and stares up at me.

'Loneliness and the feeling of being unwanted is the most terrible poverty of all,' she says. 'So if we can give them nothing else we give them love, to show them they are not forgotten.'

'What makes you do this?' I ask her. She leans closer and speaks very quietly, almost in a whisper.

'Years ago, when I was on a train to Darjeeling, I felt Jesus telling me to serve him by helping the poorest of the poor.' Her eyes stare deep into mine.

And then she adds, 'To me, each one of those poor people is Jesus in disguise.'

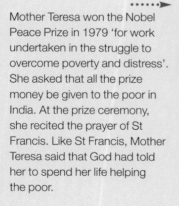

Mother Teresa won the Nobel Peace Prize in 1979 'for work undertaken in the struggle to overcome poverty and distress'. She asked that all the prize money be given to the poor in India. At the prize ceremony, she recited the prayer of St Francis. Like St Francis, Mother Teresa said that God had told her to spend her life helping the poor.

Mother Teresa cares for orphans at her Sishu Bhavan (Children's Home). The children were brought there from the streets of Kolkata (Calcutta).

Mother Teresa shows love for the poorest

Mother Teresa first came to India when she was nineteen. She was shocked by the poverty and despair in the faces of people gazing up at her from the street doorways and cardboard shelters. A few years later she gave up working as a teacher in a convent school to go out into the slums on her own to see how she could help. By the end of her life over 4,000 of Mother Teresa's followers were working for poor, sick and dying people around the world.

'Do not wait for leaders; do it alone, person to person.'
Mother Teresa

Who are the Missionaries of Charity?

Mother Teresa started an order of nuns called the Missionaries of Charity. 'Charity' is the word used by Christians for loving kindness shown to other people. 'Giving money to charity' means giving for the benefit of others. Mother Teresa's efforts provided shelter for thousands of the sick and dying, and ensured that thousands of children were cared for and given foster parents.

MARTIN LUTHER KING

WHO WAS MARTIN LUTHER KING?

Martin Luther King lived **1929–1968**

He was born **Michael King, Jr** but his father changed his son's name in honour of Martin Luther (see p. 62)

In which country? **USA**

Where? **America**

Religious association **Christianity**

Quality **Dignity**: King said 'Let no man pull you low enough to hate him.'

After his historic speech in front of a huge crowd in Washington, DC, 1963, Martin Luther King met President Kennedy at the White House.

'*We must learn to live together as brothers or perish together as fools.*'
Martin Luther King

Martin Luther King was an inspirational campaigner for black civil rights in America. He was a Baptist Church minister, who believed that non-violent resistance to unfair laws would win equality and dignity for black people everywhere.

'*Life's most urgent question is: what are you doing for others?*'
Martin Luther King

EQUALS **FREEDOM**

WE DEMAND EQUAL RIGHTS NOW!

WE MARCH FOR INTEGRATED SCHOOLS NOW!

WE DEMAND DECENT HOUSING NOW!

WE DEMAND AN END TO BIAS NOW!

WE AN END POLICE BRUTALITY NOW!

FREEDOM

FREEDOM IN '63

Martin Luther King tells Americans he has a dream for the future

Martin Luther King is about to speak to a huge crowd, who want to be treated equally, and not by different sets of laws according to their colour.

It is the largest public gathering in the history of the USA. Over a quarter of a million people have come to the Washington Monument in the nation's capital for a major protest march. They are holding placards and banners with these words on them – 'Equal Rights Now!', 'Freedom', and 'We March For Voting Rights'. One of their leaders is a preacher called Martin Luther King.

Martin Luther King grew up in Georgia, one of America's southern states, where now, in 1963, black people live separately from white people and have to go to different schools, different shops, and different parks. They even have to sit separately on buses. Black workers are paid less than white workers, and if you have black skin you are not allowed to vote in elections. Martin Luther King believes it is God's mission for him to fight against all this unfairness.

The people are so excited that they start marching before it is time. They surge up the National Mall linking arms and singing 'We shall overcome!' Most of the protesters are black but about a quarter are white, and many have painted an equals sign (like this =) on their forehead as a symbol of equality.

People taking part in the famous March on Washington in 1963 wanted 'Equal Rights' (the same laws for everybody). They also wanted 'Integrated Schools' – for black and white children to be allowed to go to the same schools – and more help for poor people. A year after this march Martin Luther King was awarded the Nobel Peace Prize.

In America black people and white people used to be forced by law to live separately. In this photograph from the 1960s, black people are only allowed to sit at the back of the bus. If there was no room on the bus, white people could stay on but black people had to walk. Martin Luther King led peaceful protests to change these laws.

There is a carnival atmosphere even though everyone is angry with the government for delaying a new law that says that black and white people must be treated equally. They feel part of something special, part of history.

The leaders take it in turns to speak to the people from a podium. The huge seated statue of Abraham Lincoln looks on. One hundred years ago it was President Lincoln who passed laws that freed all the black slaves in America. And yet today their descendants are still having to fight their government for their basic human rights.

After some speeches, prayers and songs it is Martin Luther King's turn. He is introduced as 'the moral leader of our country', and people cheer.

'Let us not seek to satisfy our thirst for freedom by drinking from the cup of bitterness and hatred,' he urges. 'We must not allow our creative protest to degenerate into physical violence.'

Martin Luther King knows the power of non-violent resistance, a tactic he learnt from the example of Mahatma Gandhi. He remembers a few months ago seeing pictures on television of the police firing water from powerful firemen's hoses at peaceful protesters and setting dogs on them. But the following month an agreement was reached to let black people to go to the same schools and restaurants and shops as white people.

He stands for a moment and looks out at the sea of people stretching all the way back to the Washington Monument. In the distance stands the great dome of the Capitol building, the seat of America's government. Martin Luther King hopes the lawmakers are listening.

The sign reads: THEY KILLED THE DREAMER BUT NOT HIS DREAM

Martin Luther King tells the crowd: 'I have a dream'

'I have a dream that one day this nation will rise up and live out the true meaning of its creed: *"We hold these truths to be self-evident: that all men are created equal."*'

'Amen!' the crowd cheer and clap.

Martin Luther King is now speaking without looking at his prepared speech. His voice shakes as if he is giving a rousing sermon.

'I have a dream that one day on the red hills of Georgia the sons of former slaves and the sons of former slave owners will be able to sit down together at a table of brotherhood.' He raises his eyes to the sky.

'I have a dream that my four children will one day live in a nation where they will not be judged by the colour of their skin but by the content of their character. I have a dream today—' he waits for the emotional applause to die down.

'I have a dream that one day right down in Alabama little black boys and black girls will be able to join hands with little white boys and white girls as sisters and brothers. I have a dream today…'

Following Gandhi's example, Martin Luther King encouraged non-violent protest. But five years after his famous speech, King was shot and killed by an assassin, just as Gandhi had been.

'Faith is taking the first step even when you don't see the whole staircase.'
Martin Luther King

DALAI LAMA

WHO IS THE DALAI LAMA?

The Dalai Lama was born in **1935**
He is also known as **Tenzin Gyatso**
In which country? **Tibet**
Where? **Asia**
Religious association **Buddhism**
Quality **Understanding**: the Dalai Lama
   understands how even our enemies are
   trying to find happiness

◄ ······

The Dalai Lama photographed at an SOS Children's Village,
which looks after children who have lost their parents because
of war, famine, or diseases like AIDS. The Dalai Lama has
helped villages in Tibet, although he hasn't been back to his
home country for over fifty years.

The Dalai Lama is the spiritual leader of the people
of Tibet. When he was only a child he was recognized
as a reincarnation of all the previous Dalai Lamas.
As the world's most famous Buddhist monk he tries to
encourage peaceful understanding and respect.

'My religion is very simple. My religion is kindness.'
Dalai Lama

'If you want to be happy, practise compassion.'
Dalai Lama

1959: The Dalai Lama escapes by night

The Dalai Lama is the spiritual leader of his country. In the 1950s many people feared a war was starting with China, and the Dalai Lama had to leave in secret.

Night has fallen in the Tibetan city of Lhasa and the Summer Palace is strangely quiet. People fear a war with China. A young man, dressed as a soldier, sits on the throne reading a book. He is reading the words of Buddha. His mother and sister and younger brother have already left, and now it is time for him to go too. He takes off his glasses and picks up a rifle. He does not want to be recognized so he does not wear his monk's robes.

The 23-year-old man is the Dalai Lama, ruler of Tibet and spiritual leader of Tibetan Buddhists. When he was two years old some monks told his parents he was the reborn spirit of the previous Dalai Lama. The Palace then became his home – until now.

A group of palace guards help him across the river where his family and friends wait. But they are not safe yet. They get onto ponies and start winding their way up the narrow track. The horseshoes clatter noisily on the stones. Suddenly they can see flickering torches behind them. Are they being followed? But it is only more of their group escaping too.

As they climb higher up the mountainside the Dalai Lama feels sick with dread. He is worried for his people, whom he has been forced to leave behind.

The Potala Palace in Tibet was the traditional winter home of the Dalai Lama. Nearby is the Summer Palace. They are in the city of Lhasa, high in the Himalayan mountains.

Photograph of Tenzin Gyatso, the young Dalai Lama, at the age of 2.

The Dalai Lama left his Tibetan home in 1959, crossing the mountains with ponies (he is the one in the middle of the picture, wearing glasses). He has not been able to return. But today he travels everywhere in the world, and many ordinary people and even world leaders listen to his advice.

But he has done what he could to prevent conflict. He followed the words of Buddha in trying to reason with the Chinese leaders with compassion and understanding. After all, they are his fellow humans, and they just want to be happy like everyone else. It is his duty to respect their happiness too. But many Tibetans have now lost patience and started a rebellion.

His pony stumbles in the dark and the Dalai Lama dismounts in order to lead it up the steep path. His companions do the same.

The next day everyone is tired. The walking is hard and they have little rest. But they must move quickly for fear of Chinese army patrols. They are trying to reach a place where the Dalai Lama could negotiate from safety. But as they trek deeper into the mountains news reaches them from Lhasa: many people have been killed and the old monasteries are in ruins. Now the Dalai Lama must flee to India.

For two weeks they pick their way across the frozen mountains, through swirling snowstorms and torrential rain, and when at last they reach the border the Dalai Lama is tired, ill, desperately sad – but safe.

He has never set foot in his beloved Tibet since then. For over 50 years he has lived in India and travelled round the world to find support for his people. He says he has tried to follow the same path of peace as Mahatma Gandhi before him. In 1989 he won the Nobel Peace Prize for his efforts.

'I am just a simple monk,' he often chuckles, his eyes twinkling. And he is still searching for a peaceful path to freedom for his people.

Six hundred years ago, the first Dalai Lama died. The head of an important monastery visited this sacred lake in Tibet. There he had a vision telling him where to look for the new Dalai Lama. Tibetans believe that today's Dalai Lama is the 14th reincarnation of a great Buddhist Master.

WHERE TO FIND OUT MORE

MOSES
The Torah is the name for the books of Moses. Shemot, or the Book of Exodus in the Old Testament of the Bible, tells the story of Moses.
MUSEUM
Beit Hatfutsot, The Museum of the Jewish People, Israel
FILMS
The Ten Commandments (directed by Cecil B. de Mille 1956)
The Prince of Egypt by Brenda Chapman, 1998

LAOZI
IMPORTANT SITES
Giant stone statue of Laozi, located at the foot of Mount Qingyuan, Fujian Province, China
Mount Sanqing, Jiangxi Province, China – a national park known as the 'Open Air Taoist Museum'
BOOK
The Legend of Lao Tzu and the Tao Te Ching by Demi, 2007

BUDDHA
IMPORTANT SITE
The birthplace of the Lord Buddha – The Mayadevi Temple, Lumbini, Nepal
MUSEUMS
London Fo Guang Temple, 84 Margaret Street, London W1, UK (www.londonfgs.org.uk). The temple organizes London's 'Birthday of Buddha' festival in May each year.
BOOK
Buddha by Demi, 1996
FILM
Little Buddha (directed by Bernardo Bertolucci, 1993)

CONFUCIUS
BOOKS
The Life and Times of Confucius by Kathleen Tracy, 2004
What Would Confucius Do? Wisdom and Advice on Achieving Success and Getting Along with Others by Evelyn Berthrong, 2005
FILM
Confucius (directed by Mei Hu, 2010)

SOCRATES
BOOKS
Socrates: Ancient Greek in Search of Truth by Pamela Dell, 2006
The Last Days of Socrates by Plato, written in the 4th century BC; Penguin Classics edition, 2003

JESUS
The life of Jesus is told in the New Testament of the Bible in the Gospels of Matthew, Mark, Luke and John.
FILMS
Ben-Hur: A Tale of The Christ (directed by William Wyler, 1959)
The Greatest Story Ever Told (directed by George Stevens, 1965)
Jesus (directed by John Krish and Peter Sykes, 1979)

MUHAMMAD
BOOKS
Muhammad of Mecca: Prophet of Islam by Elsa Marston, 2001
The Life of the Prophet Muhammad by Leila Azzam and Aisha Gouverneur, 1985
FILM
The Message (US title: *Mohammad, Messenger of God*) (directed by Moustapha Akkad, 1977)

ST FRANCIS
BOOK
St Francis of Assisi: The Patron Saint of Animals by Lucy Lethbridge, 2005
WEBSITE
www.franciscan-archive.org/patriarcha

DOGEN
BOOK
One Hand Clapping: Zen Stories For All Ages by Junko Morimoto, 1995
FILM
Zen (directed by Banmei Takahashi, 2009. Japanese with English subtitles)

RUMI
BOOKS
Tales from Rumi edited by Ali Fuat Bilkan, 2000
Selected Poems by Rumi and Coleman Barks, 2004
WEBSITE
www.rumi.net

JOAN OF ARC
MUSEUM
Musée Jeanne d'Arc, 33 place du Vieux Marché, 76000 Rouen, France
BOOK
Personal Recollections of Joan of Arc by Mark Twain, 1896
FILM
Joan of Arc (directed by V. Fleming, 1948)
PLAY
Saint Joan by George Bernard Shaw, first performed 1923
GAME
Jeanne d'Arc for Sony Playstation Portable (PSP)

GURU NANAK
MUSEUM
Guru Nanak Sikh Museum, 9 Holy Bones, Leicester, UK
BOOK
The Book of Nanak by Navtej Sarna

MARTIN LUTHER
MUSEUM
Collegienstrasse 54, Lutherstadt Wittenberg, Germany
BOOK
Courage and Conviction: Chronicles of the Reformation Church by Mindy and Brandon Withrow, 2009 – includes a chapter on Martin Luther.
FILM
Luther (directed by Eric Till, 2003)
WEBSITE
www.martinluther.de

CHIEF SEATTLE
MUSEUM
Suquamish Museum and Cultural Center, 15838 Sandy Hook Road, Poulsbo, Washington State, USA
BOOK
The World of Chief Seattle: How Can One Sell The Air? by Warren Jefferson, 2001
WEBSITE
www.suquamish.org

BAHA'U'LLAH
MAGAZINE
Brilliant Star (6 issues per year about the Baha'i world, for children) www.brilliantstarmagazine.org
WEBSITE
www.bahai.org.uk

MAHATMA GANDHI
MUSEUM
National Gandhi Museum, Rajghat, New

Delhi 110002 www.gandhimuseum.org
WEBSITE
www.gandhi-manibhavan.org
FILM
Gandhi (directed by Richard
Attenborough, 1982)
Look on www.youtube.com for lots of
film clips.
BOOK
Gandhi by Amy Pastan, 2006

HAILE SELASSIE
WEBSITE
www.bbc.co.uk/religion/religions/rastafa
ri/beliefs/haileselassie.shtml
VIDEOS
See www.youtube.com and similar
sites, such as Google Videos, and
www.rastaites.com/Videos/selassie.htm

MOTHER TERESA
FILM
*Mother Teresa: In The Name Of God's
Poor* (directed by Kevin Connor, 1997)

Mother Teresa (directed by Anne and
Jeannette Petrie, 1986)
Look on www.youtube.com for lots of
film clips.
BOOK
A Simple Path by Mother Teresa, 1995
*Mother Teresa: A Photographic Story of a
Life* by Maya Gold, 2008
MUSEUM
Memorial House of Mother Teresa in
Skopje, Macedonia
www.memorialhouseofmotherteresa.org

MARTIN LUTHER KING
FILM
Martin Luther King's speeches, including
his world-famous 'I Have a Dream'
speech, can be seen on
www.youtube.com together with lots
of other film clips.
MUSEUMS
National Civil Rights Museum, 450
Mulberry Street, Memphis, Tennessee,
USA (www.civilrightsmuseum.org)

WEBSITE
www.thekingcenter.org
The King Center, 449 Auburn Avenue,
NE, Atlanta, Georgia, USA
BOOK
*I Have a Dream: Writings and Speeches
That Changed the World* by Martin
Luther King Jr., 1992

DALAI LAMA
Interviews and speeches can be seen on
www.youtube.com
BOOK
*Boy on the Lion Throne: The Childhood
of the 14th Dalai Lama* by Elizabeth
Cody, 2009
FILM
Kundun (directed by Martin Scorsese,
1997)
DOCUMENTARY
Tibet: Cry of the Snow Lion (directed by
Tom Piozet, 2002)

PICTURE CREDITS

Key: **a** = above **b** = below **l** = left **r** = right

INDEX

ABOUT THE AUTHOR

Henry Whitbread is a freelance writer. He studied Theology and Religious Studies at Cambridge University. He has three children.